Also by Morton Shulman

Anyone Can Make a Million
Billion Dollar Windfall
Coroner
Anyone Can Still Make a Million
Anyone Can Make Big Money Buying Art
Member of the Legislature

How to
Invest Your
Money &
Profit from
INFLATION

How to Invest Your Money & Profit from INFLATION

Morton Shulman

Random House · *New York*

Copyright © 1979, 1980 by Morton Shulman

All rights reserved under International and Pan-American Copyright
Conventions. Published in the United States by Random House, Inc.,
New York. Originally published in Canada by Hurtig Publishers in 1979.
Limited, Toronto. Originally published in Canada by Hurtig Publishers.

Library of Congress Cataloging in Publication Data
Shulman, Morton.
How to invest your money & profit from inflation.
1. Investments.   2. Inflation (Finance)
I. Title.
HG4521.S3579   332.6′78   79-26319
ISBN 0-394-51064-X

Manufactured in the United States of America

24689753

Contents

Introduction

The world today is seeing a redistribution of wealth that is greater than anything since the French Revolution. After fifty years of growing affluence, the ordinary citizen is now seeing a slippage in his standard of living. Every year he makes more money, but finds that it buys fewer goods. Because of inflation, "solid" investments like government bonds yield less than the loss in their true value. The majority of the population is getting a little poorer every year. But this general attrition in buying ability does not affect everyone. A few people are keeping up with inflation and a handful are jumping far ahead of it.

How to Invest Your Money and Profit from Inflation is an explanation of methods whereby the investor with moderate resources can learn techniques that will preserve capital and living standards in the inflationary spiral that in recent years has been so rapid.

How much do you need to start investing profitably today?

For $50, you can buy a 200-year-old painting.
For $57.89, you can buy a 1927 Lindbergh.
For $175, you can buy a case of 1970 Palmer.
For $380, you can buy one Krugerrand.
For $400, you can buy 100 Welkom.
For $500, you can buy 1,000 German marks.
For $700, you can buy 100 Southvaal.
For $1,000, you can buy a Samurai bond.
For $1,000, you can buy one share in a commodity fund.
For $1,000, you can buy a unit in an offshore fund.
For $3,000, you can sell one GNMA.
For $10,000, you can open a commodity account.
For $100,000, you can buy one share in an oil-drilling fund.

All of these and many, many other methods of profiting from inflation are described in this book.

My credentials for writing this book are simple enough. I saw the inflation coming and publicized it long before most economists or politicians spoke out. In 1966, in my first book, I predicted the devaluation of the U.S. dollar, and I advised everyone with money to load up on gold at $35 per ounce. In 1973 I wrote *Anyone Can Still Make a Million* advising the purchase of silver at $1.40 and saying, "I predict that this price ($1.40) will multiply many times over the next few years." Time has proven me right—and I have personally profited from my observations.

M.S.

How to
Invest Your
Money &
Profit from
INFLATION

The Old Virtues Are Dead

———————◆•◆———————

My father was a life insurance salesman and the company for which he worked distributed a pamphlet called *Save for a Rainy Day*. Dad tried to instill the precepts from that little booklet in our home:

- Don't buy anything you can't afford.
- Savings are essential before beginning any investment program.
- Life insurance is the best form of investment.
- Don't borrow money.
- Don't speculate, but if you must, then buy a mortgage.
- Don't buy real estate. It's better to rent.
- Government bonds are the safest place to put your money.

That philosophy made sense in the thirties, but it has proven a trap for so many people who grew up in those depressed days. Anyone following my father's advice today would be headed straight towards economic disaster because of inflation.

It is very hard to accept that all the old "safe" investments, the type that bankers suggested for widows and orphans and all those who couldn't afford to lose their money, are now certain to produce losses. Not losses in terms of number of dollars, but losses where it *really* counts: in *buying power*. It is not easy to stop thinking in terms of the number of dollars you earn, even though it is no longer a constant concept. When I was a young doctor I earned $20,000 a year and thought I was rich. Now I earn many times that and have no greater buying power with my salary alone than I had twenty years ago. The problem is that few wage earners can keep up with inflation by increases in salary.

As I write this chapter, the current inflation rate is 12% per annum. An increase in my salary of 12% will not hold me even, not only because I must pay the full 12% increase in prices, but because I do not receive the full 12% increase in salary. The reason of course is income tax. If you are in the 50% income bracket, you must get a 24% raise just to stay even during 12% inflation.

And don't be fooled by the figures given out by the government purporting to show the inflation rate, since the Consumer Price Index consistently understates the true inflation rate. In September 1979 the government said prices were going up at a rate of about 12½% per year, but any housewife visiting the supermarket could see that prices were a heck of a lot more than 12½% higher than last year.

This trickery is done by excluding certain costs from the C.P.I. For example, Social Security taxes are included, but not income tax—and so when President Carter pondered a tax cut for 1980, his advisers recommended a cut in Social Security taxes but not in Income Tax because this would help lower the "rate of inflation." Same final effect—but the C.P.I. would be lower! It's pure flimflam.

How does this situation affect traditional investments?

Government Bonds

What could be safer than a loan to the government of your country backed by the full resources of the nation's treasury? Let us consider just such an investment, one of the most common made in the United States today. Suppose that one year ago you had taken $1,000 and bought a government savings bond paying 8½% interest. Today your bond is still worth $1,000 and to boot you have received $85 interest. But the $1,085 you have today will not buy as much as your original $1,000 would have bought one year ago. And of course, in addition, you must pay tax to the government on your $85 "profit."

What has happened is that in this "safe" investment you have taken a *real* loss. It is all part of a huge con. Governments still issue such bonds, and banks, brokers and trust companies conspire to sell them in the name of safety and good return on capital—neither of which the investor in bonds receives. After a decade of rapid inflation, I would have thought that the public would have awakened to this fact, but they have not. Most investors still fall for the same fraud in which they have been robbed steadily and repeatedly by our governments.

And what of the foolish person who buys a government bond and keeps it ten years till maturity? At today's rate of accelerating inflation, the relatively solid $1,000 you invest today that now will buy a motorcycle will probably not even purchase a bicycle in ten years.

Don't buy government bonds!

Corporation Bonds

Corporation bonds are not really different from government bonds. The only variation is that in this case you are lending your money to a corporation rather than to a government. The corporation usually pays about 1% or 2% more interest because of the possible danger of the company's going broke. But here again there is no way that the interest paid will keep up with the rate of inflation.[1]

Don't buy corporation bonds!

Life Insurance

Investment in life insurance is an even worse place to put money than bonds. Even in stable times, buying expensive insurance is a losing proposition because one must outlive the insurance in order to get back the savings. In inflationary times, it becomes a hopeless trap.

Term insurance, for protection only, may cost $5 for $1,000 worth of insurance for one year. Insurance combined with a savings plan may cost $35 for one year, with the extra $30 plus interest to be returned in twenty years. With today's inflation, those savings will be worthless in twenty years. I find it amazing that millions of these savings-plan policies are sold every year, in spite of the fact that all purchasers will lose their entire savings. In 1966, as

---

[1] Convertible bonds are a different situation. I'll discuss these later.

inflation was barely under way, I wrote an essay on life insurance that is even more true today. Then the only riposte of the insurance companies was that savings insurance forced those persons to save who otherwise would never do it. Perhaps that was true then. Today they should be encouraged *not* to save.

Don't buy life or savings-plan insurance!

Mortgages

The purchaser of a mortgage is making exactly the same mistake as the purchaser of a bond, except that instead of lending his money to a government or a corporation, he is lending it to an individual and the security is a house instead of a government's treasury or a company's assets. Mortgages usually run for five or ten years and the interest rate depends on the risk. It has all the disadvantages of a bond plus the added problem of not being able to liquidate for many years. In today's financial climate, mortgages are sure to produce losses in buying power.

Don't buy mortgages!

Bad Investment Advice

The reason so many people hold such poor investments is the vast quantity of bad advice given so freely. Last year I hosted a television show on investment, with a panel consisting of a lady who had written a book on investment,[2] the president of a stock exchange, a senior member of the investment dealers' association and an associate editor of *Fortune* magazine. My first question to the panel was to ask

[2] Alix Granger, *Investing Profitably in Canada* (Vancouver: J. J. Douglas, 1975).

where they would advise a widow with $100,000 to invest. The lady adviser and the investment dealer recommended government bonds, and the other two panelists refused my suggestion that they should disagree with this advice. Yet when I chastised the panel off-camera, they all volunteered that *none* of their own money was in bonds, but that "widows want security."

I am a contributing editor to a company that sells a course on investing to the public. In the fall of 1979 the general manager of the company requested me to write a lesson on inflation for their clients and gave me an outline to follow, which began: "When to use bonds and other fixed-income investments." I was quite surprised, but when I suggested to him that there was no place for this type of investment during an inflation, he replied, "Morty, I know you're right, but there are some people who just can't sleep if their money is in gold or real estate or stocks or anything that fluctuates. Their psyche requires the security of a bond and it's our job to advise them as best we can. You have to give this older-type investor someplace to put his money where he feels that he has safety of capital."

It is true that all the traditional books on investment advice start off by saying that the three qualities to look for in any investment are, in order of importance:

(1) safety of capital
(2) yield
(3) possibility of capital appreciation

The hardest possible thing for an investor to accept is that there is no longer *any investment* that will guarantee safety of capital and the traditional ways in which such safety was sought; bonds, life insurance or mortgages not only fail to give safety, they guarantee a loss of true capital. In today's economic climate, there are no risk-free investments.

Worse, there is no way of getting a yield, since there is no investment available in the United States today which gives any yield at all. It is true that stocks and bonds give dividends and pay interest ranging from 2% to 10% per year, but in no single case does this yield exceed the inflation rate. Thus, investing in a bond paying 8% with the inflation rate at 12% shows not only no true yield, but a real loss of 4% at the end of the year. In fact, the loss is even greater than this, since part of the existing "interest" actually goes to taxes.

The result of our inflation is that neither safety of capital nor yield is possible and we must instead look to the third factor, capital appreciation, because it is our only hope of keeping up. Those foolish persons who say that they only "sleep well" when their money is in the bank or in government bonds are going to end up losing a lot more than sleep before 1984 arrives.

A Little
Inflation History

Our inflation began with Franklin D. Roosevelt and the brilliant English economist John Maynard Keynes. In 1932 the United States was in the midst of a terrible depression. Millions were unemployed and bankruptcies were dragging down company after company. The stores were full of goods, but no one had money to buy them. Production was grinding to a halt, resulting in even more unemployment. It was the ultimate vicious circle.

Following Keynes' advice, Roosevelt pumped paper money into circulation, which for the first time in U.S. history was not backed by gold. In fact, the U.S. greenbacks were simply IOUs. The American President set up artificial work programs like the WPA, which put the unemployed to work clearing forests, paving roads, or even painting pictures, and paid them with paper money, which they in turn used to buy goods. In time, this produced a demand that set the factories to work again. The factories hired men to produce goods, and so the depression cycle was broken.

It worked exactly as Keynes had predicted, and by the time World War II was over, prosperity had returned to the United States and the world. The dark cloud overhanging this prosperity was the rapidly increasing amount of U.S. paper money circulating with no set value behind it. Its worth depended only upon the value the world believed was behind each dollar, and every year there were more dollars.

Aware of this problem, Keynes suggested that when good times returned, the government should use its increased revenues to retire the extra paper money printed during the Depression. But this turned out to be the great flaw in the plan, for it became impossible to cut back on government spending. In 1941, just at the point when the attempt to cut expenses should have been made, the United States plunged into war, and after the war the federal government instituted a whole series of welfare schemes in order to prevent recession and voter displeasure. These ranged all the way from farm support programs to outright welfare, from food subsidies to cash grants to the arts. The net result of this was to push the federal deficit higher each successive year. And the final culmination was the war, with its huge expenditures.

Clever economists recognized the financial trap, but politicians found it impossible to cut back. In a democracy, every election is a competition for votes, and that competition is invariably won by the person or the party that promises (and sometimes delivers) the most to the largest number of people. The electorate is basically selfish. They will vote for lowering taxes (for example, Proposition 13) and increasing benefits. They will never and have never voted for increasing taxes or cutting back on services.

For two decades the results of this blitz of paper were quite pleasant. Social services expanded manifold, wages rose, and every year politicians were able to give the people more and more presents without increasing taxes. Of course, there was some inflation, but as late as 1966 it was running at only 3% annually in the United States, and at that rate it didn't hurt anyone. Well, almost no one: pensioners on very limited incomes did feel the pinch, but they didn't matter too much. They were old enough to die off before they got badly hurt, and more important, they were not organized politically and so they were ignored by politicians of all parties.

In addition, until 1969 the United States shielded itself from most of the inflation by exporting it. From 1945 on, the United States government printed vast quantities of paper money, which were shipped abroad in return for French wine, German cars, Italian motorcycles and Japanese television sets. This process came a cropper in 1969 when the overseas world suddenly realized they were awash in U.S. green. That was the year much of the money came home. The French bought U.S. gold, the Russians bought wheat, and the Japanese arrived with suitcases of money and traveled across North America buying up Impressionist art. This sudden influx of paper money into the U.S. economy gave inflation a big impetus. As prices began to rise, unions demanded higher wages, and various pressure groups pushed for more welfare for the poor. Neither American political party was able to withstand the welfare pressure and even so-called conservatives joined in the rush to further damage the economy by printing more money "to help the disadvantaged."

Politicians pay lip service to restricting the money supply, but no one ever takes this very seriously. I relate, with some pride as a Canadian, the difference between Canada and the United States in this regard. In 1969 inflation in Canada had reached 4%. The leaders of the two opposition parties, David Lewis and Robert Stanfield, were campaigning across Canada, inveighing against our easy money policies. Prime Minister Trudeau noted the increasing newspaper coverage and announced in a major speech that inflation had to be tackled and that the government was therefore raising interest rates and restricting the money supply. The inevitable followed, and as money became more expensive to borrow, companies restricted expansion, unemployment began to grow (to 5% of the work force) and mortgages on homes became more expensive.

The same two opposition leaders now began giving speeches decrying the results of the tight-money policy and warning that Trudeau's policies were certain to produce a depression. The newspapers followed with huge stories and warning editorials, and after ninety days the pressure on Trudeau from his backbenchers became so intense that he gave in and completely reversed his monetary policies. He made the best of the situation by announcing that "inflation has been beaten" and therefore tight money was no longer necessary.

The reason I relate this story with pride is that several years later when Gerald Ford became President, his first speech was to warn that the great danger facing the United States was inflation. It took him only four days to reverse himself and say that really the greatest danger was unemployment and so the country must follow easy money policies. In Canada the reversal had taken ninety days: Canadians have staying power!

As we entered the 1970's the inflation rate climbed above 5% and now the U.S. government experimented with price and wage controls even though dozens of other nations in similar circumstances had tried that route and had failed.

The reason for the failure of price controls is obvious. To take a simple example, suppose you are a manufacturer of candy bars which you sell for 15¢ and the government passes a law saying you can't sell them for more than 15¢. All might go well for a brief period, until you discover that one of the ingredients of your candy, cocoa, which must be imported, has jumped in price to the extent that you can no longer manufacture your bars and make a profit. As you stop producing, a shortage of candy bars follows. The same situation applies to every manufactured commodity.

Price control invariably leads to shortages because no nation is self-sufficient and inflation is world-wide. Shortages lead to black markets, for there is always someone prepared to take the risks and fill the demand for a price.

It doesn't matter how severe are the measures proposed to punish breakers of the price-control laws. During World War II we had penalties sufficiently serious that black marketeers could be locked up "for the duration," and in addition to the penalties, we were able to appeal to patriotism. Despite these factors, there was a flourishing black market in gasoline coupons and in tires, and apartment "key money" became the rule. Laws can't prevent black markets. They can only drive up the price.

After a brief interval the United States abandoned the price control system because it didn't work. By 1978 the inflation rate had climbed to 9%. This was probably the last chance to stop the inflationary process, for once the rate becomes double digit, 10% or over, it feeds on itself. At this point, the steady rise in prices becomes obvious to

every shopper, and individuals and groups attempt to protect themselves by grabbing for even higher wages. However, higher wages can never keep up with the rise of
inflation, and in fact, the struggle to keep ahead increases
the rate of the inflationary spiral.

Analyzing a Classic Inflation: Germany 1914 to 1923

———◆•◆———

Most of the bad financial advice given today is not a result of fraud but rather of ignorance—ignorance of the past. Many nations have undergone inflation before us and all have followed the same basic pattern. It is surprising how few of our politicians have studied other inflations, and as a result, the most amazing misconceptions abound.

In October 1977 a short-lived paper called *Magazine of Wall Street* ran adjacent articles by two self-styled experts. One said that during the great German inflation, holders of stocks suffered a relative loss of buying power, while the other said exactly the opposite. It is invaluable to our understanding of our own inflationary times to analyze what actually happened in this classic inflation.

Fortunately, everything that occurred during the inflation in Germany has been recorded. Economics Professor Bresciani-Turroni worked with the Reparations Commission in Germany throughout the catastrophe. As the head of Export Control, he carefully recorded the month-by-month changes in the value of everything—stocks, bonds, mortgages, foreign exchange, etc. He published his classic study in 1932 in Italy, and it was translated into English and published by the firm of Augustus Kelley in London in 1937 under the title of *The Economics of Inflation*. I don't think any book is of greater value today.

Germany suffered inflation for similar reasons to ours: government overspending. They, too, began their waste with a war, but the culmination did not come because of welfare programs but rather because of the huge reparation payments Germany was forced to pay to the victorious nations after the war.

The basis of the inflation began on July 31, 1914, when the Reichsbank suspended the conversion of paper marks into gold. It ended on November 15, 1923, when the mark had sunk so low that one U.S. dollar could purchase a trillion German marks. On that day citizens were given one new gold mark for every *trillion* old marks they held! Between those two events, the following had occurred.

For the first five years inflation went relatively slowly, with the amount of money in circulation quadrupling, the cost of living doubling and the price of gold and the U.S. dollar rising by only 50%. Then, in the sixth year, gold and the dollar soared, more than doubling in the one year, while the cost of living and the money in circulation rose by another 50%. From 1919 to 1920 there occurred a characteristic common to all inflation: a massive rush to buy gold and foreign exchange. Gold went up 1,500% in the one year while the cost of imported goods rose by 1,900%. In the final phases of inflation, from 1922 to 1923, imported goods and gold rose by 22,000%, domestic goods rose by 18,000% and food by 14,000%.

According to Bresciani-Turroni, the sudden collapse of the mark was due to psychological influences—a lack of confidence in the future of Germany and a desire to avoid the heavy taxes with which the government belatedly hoped to balance its budget. It is significant to the United States that in February 1923 Germany announced various measures to support the foreign exchange value of the mark (including making illegal the holding of gold and foreign currency), but at the same time the government continued the printing of paper money and deficit financing. The law was almost totally ignored. In an effort to support the mark, the Reichsbank made a daily sale of 20 million gold marks by auction, the only result being that the gold was gone and the mark continued to sink.

The German government was reluctant to raise interest rates for fear that this would cause a further rise in prices and unemployment. Instead they tried to ration credit, only the "more deserving firms" being given this honor. This resulted in tremendous enrichment of these few lucky companies. At the end, this policy had to be discontinued, and interest rates rose finally to 30% per day.

One odd offshoot of the inflation was that at first prices were going up faster than the exchange rate. It became profitable for Germans to travel to other countries, buy goods there and resell them in Germany. This in turn further depressed the value of the mark. As time went on, the mark gradually ceased to be a "store of value" and savings more and more were converted into gold or foreign currency.

As the mark began to fall rapidly, unemployment fell with it, and by the summer of 1922 unemployment practically disappeared. With the depreciation of the mark, foreign and home demand for goods grew. Foreigners wanted to profit by the greater purchasing power of their money in Germany and Germans were anxious to buy hard goods to get rid of their depreciating paper money. If North America follows the same scenario, unemployment should be down considerably in 1980 from 1979. However, in late 1979 the U.S. government massively raised interest rates, and this will cause a temporary rise in unemployment.

From 1919 to 1923 there was a redistribution of wealth in Germany, with a few entrepreneurs becoming tremendously rich. Because of rent control, real rents fell to almost zero, allowing employers to reduce nominal wages accordingly. Owners of rental property could no longer afford repair or taxes and many abandoned their properties.

The inflation so restricted the real income of many classes of consumers that later their demand for consumption goods fell. As an example, a glut of milk developed despite falling production because the young families who normally purchase milk could no longer afford it. On the other hand, there was a tremendous boom in the manufacture of machines and the building of factories.

There was a vast increase in unproductive labor due to the complex calculations required in every trade, the continual conversions into foreign exchange, the application of complicated taxes, the computation of pay supplements and the numerous economic controls. An actual shortage of bookkeepers developed. The ratio of office employees to production workers rose by 42% in nine years. Associated with this, was a decline in the productivity of labor because of the diminution of real wages associated with a decline in the will to work. Many workmen found themselves just as well off not working. Productivity fell by close to 50%.

At first stock prices kept up with inflation, but after four years they fell far behind. By 1922 stock prices had increased 89 times in price, while gold had gone up 1,525 times and the consumer price index increased 945 times. This catastrophic drop in share prices produced strange situations. For example, all the share capital of the Daimler car company was priced at the value of only 327 Daimler cars. Corporations reacted to this turn of events by creating special voting shares so as to protect control of their company. The reason stocks failed to keep up was that on December 1, 1921, the public was badly hit by a selling spree on the stock exchange, and from that point, people became convinced that the only sure way to protect their savings was with gold or foreign exchange.

As Bresciani-Turroni put it:

Expressed in paper marks the prices of shares seemed high. This exercised a psychological influence on the great mass of shareholders. Deluded by the apparently high prices, even the most cautious shareholders were induced to sell their securities; and only much later, when the veil of inflation had been torn aside, did they realize that they had made a very bad bargain.

In the final phases of the inflation, stock prices again surged upwards because of the difficulty in obtaining gold, and some shares actually became overvalued.

Another characteristic phenomenon of the inflation was the lessening of the differences between wages of different groups, skilled and unskilled, young and old, men and women. This was because as unskilled workers' wages reached only subsistence levels, they were perforce increased, while the real wages of skilled workers were allowed to fall.

Stockholders who held their shares throughout the inflation lost 75% of their original investments. Mortgage and bondholders lost everything. In 1925 the German government passed a law revaluing mortgages and debentures to 25% of their original gold value, but it proved almost totally impossible to enforce. Homeowners who lived in their homes saved the investment in their homes and did not have to pay off the mortgage, but tenants fared even better, living for several years almost rent-free.

The group most seriously hurt by inflation was the professionals, especially doctors, whose true incomes fell by three-quarters. In comparison, government employees lost 50%. Consumption of better-quality meats fell while that of horses and dogs soared. Open prostitution increased as did the number of pawnshops.

It all ended in 1923, when the mark became worthless and the government was forced back to gold to guarantee their new currency. In the aftermath came a credit crunch, 10% unemployment and a severe depression, followed by Adolf Hitler—but that is outside the province of this book. What we must decide is how much of this scenario applies to us today.

Can Inflation Be Stopped?

————•••————

The United States in 1980 is not like Germany of 1919. The United States is powerful where Germany was weak. It has considerable reserves and borrowing power and has many more options open to it. Often I hear the comment "I'm not worried. The government will solve our problems if they get bad enough. They have the tools to do it."

Obviously, all the advice in this book is worthless if some genius comes along and stops inflation and the slide of the dollar. Is this possible? The answer is an unequivocal *no, it is not possible.*

It is not individual or corporate spending that has driven us into inflation. It is governments who year after year have spent billions more than they have received and who in order to reverse this process must grossly cut their expenditures. But how do they do this? It is generally agreed that any massive cut in welfare will result in politically unacceptable violence in cities like New York.

Just as important, it is probably equally impossible for

governments to encourage productivity when for two generations they have encouraged profligacy. People in government talk about increasing productivity but they don't mean themselves or their own employees. The crazy thing is that while we have encouraged industry to produce more—for example, it is great if a way can be found to increase one worker's output in a refrigerator factory from 31 refrigerators per week to 32—no one dares suggest increasing the number of students in each teacher's class from 31 to 32.

The gradual loss of productivity in government is well illustrated in my home of Ontario. The present "Conservative" government came to power in 1943 when there were 2,300 civil servants in the province. Today we are governed, not particularly better, by 80,000 civil servants. Periodically, the government itself becomes alarmed at the increase in the number of its employees and puts a halt to hiring. But somehow the number of employees continues to grow as departments hire those people they think they need "by contract," instead of making them actual civil servants.

Last year the number of students enrolling in the schools fell drastically. As a result, there was a surplus of teachers. Rather than fire the extra teachers, the teachers' union and a group of popularity-seeking school trustees urged that instead we take this "great opportunity to raise standards" by decreasing the size of classes!

Government resolve re inflation has now so weakened that the minutes of the U.S. Federal Reserve Open Market Committee for July 18, 1978, read as follows:

It was emphasized that the high rate of inflation in prospect for the quarters immediately ahead was attributable in part to government actions and to some strong forces in the private sector—including the effects of the depreciation of the dollar—that were likely to be moderated appreciably by the stance of monetary policy. In these circumstances, it was argued, the committee ought to raise the upper limit of the range for Ml [paper money supply] to allow for a growth rate that—given upward cost pressures on prices—was more nearly consistent with the generally anticipated rate of growth in real and nominal GNP for the year ahead and that, consequently, was more likely to be achieved.

It could have come straight from the Reichsbank minister in 1921: "We can't stop the inflation anyway, so let's print more paper money to increase growth rate."

The U.S. Federal Reserve is the body which is supposed to control inflation and to stop the growth in money supply. As *The Wall Street Journal* described it, on August 30, 1978:

> Over the past few years the stated policy of the Federal Reserve has been to combat inflation by gradually slowing money growth. In practice, fear of political fallout from every blip in short-term interest rates has so gripped the Fed that it has not succeeded in turning this rhetoric into policy. Money growth has not slowed but accelerated. Now we have reached the point where even the rhetoric is challenged, where governors of the Federal Reserve offer a counsel of surrender.

These words foretell our financial doom. No politician is able to stop this inflation. No one in the United States is going to save the nation's financial health. All people can do is to protect their own finances so as to preserve the standard of living of their families.

It is fascinating that in late 1979, even as the Federal Reserve was raising interest rates, the money supply continued to increase rapidly. This portends bad news for the 1980's.

What Is the U.S. Government Doing About the Fall of the Dollar?

For many years the American government just ignored the exchange rate of the U.S. dollar as it gradually sank. The Secretary of the Treasury in 1977 even expressed his pleasure at this trend, saying it made American goods more competitive and reduced unemployment. Finally in October 1978, President Carter proclaimed that he intended to strengthen the U.S. dollar. He would auction off the U.S. gold reserve at the rate of 1,500,000 ounces per month. *The Wall Street Journal* called it the last throw of the dice.

I'd love to know who advised that crazy course of action. If the dollar is weak now with the gold in Frot Knox, *how* can it possibly be strengthened by selling off all of the only acceptable international currency belonging to the United States? It's exactly the same as a man going broke by overspending, who announces that he intends to continue his expenditures but will solve his problem by selling his house. When the money from the house is gone, what does he do?

After Carter has sold the gold, he can try the various steps that Germany tried during its inflation. An obvious move would be to impose foreign exchange controls, forbidding U.S. citizens from owning gold or foreign currencies and restricting the amount of money carried by tourists. This would not solve the basic problem of government overspending, but it certainly would put off the day of final reckoning if these activities are curtailed.

In peacetime, however, such controls have never worked because enforcement is too difficult. Indeed, such controls might have just the opposite results. They could initiate a wave of smuggling of currency out of the country for deposit in Switzerland, Germany or Japan. Just a rumor of such controls in Canada in 1978 started a rush to export funds. As a result, hundreds of millions of dollars from Canada were invested in the United States and overseas.

Certainly an army of civil servants would be needed to enforce these new regulations. Everyone crossing the border would have to be searched and every letter going overseas would have to be opened. If the Mexican border can't be sealed to illegal immigrants, how can the entire United States be sealed to currency? I don't think the U.S. administration is stupid enough to try it. But if they do, it won't work.

Another route would be to follow the Canadian example and borrow vast amounts of foreign currency with which to purchase U.S. funds. This would temporarily sustain the trading price of the U.S. dollar. One hopes this would be done more intelligently than in Canada, where 7 billion U.S. dollars, borrowed at an average of 8%, were used to prop up the Canadian dollar. Simultaneously, the Canadian government lent several billion dollars interest free to Third World countries as Canada's contribution to world development.

Such a policy won't work even in the short term, because the borrowed money is soon gone (it went at the rate of $300 million a month in Canada) and the borrowing country is left owing the foreign currency—which must be repaid someday—and this in its turn forces the dollar lower. When the Canadian government began borrowing to sustain the dollar, it stood at 89¢ U.S. Seven months and $2 billion later, it had fallen below 85¢. The United States might try such a strategy, but it won't help.

A third option would be to impose strict import controls and drastically reduce the importation of foreign goods. This would rupture the U.S. foreign trade treaties and almost certainly produce a world-wide depression which could not be kept out of the United States. No, there is not much chance that this mistake will take place, either.

There was one step that President Carter took that helped matters, at least temporarily. At the end of 1978 he ordered a *massive* raising of interest rates.

With interest rates lower than the inflation rate, as they were throughout 1978, it made economic sense for speculators to borrow money to buy assets. This sped up the inflation, and the government realized that if it were to make money very expensive by raising the prime rate by several percentage points, it would become more difficult for borrowers and there would be some inflow of foreign currency to take advantage of the high interest. The effect is only temporary, but the U.S. government tried this because it had so few other options. Higher interest rates, however, inevitably result in recession and high unemployment. Thus, the government will be tempted to lower interest rates temporarily in 1980 in preparation for the November elections, and this will result in reacceleration of inflation.

How and when will inflation end? Every nation that has undergone prolonged serious inflation has seen it end in the same way, with an economic and political collapse.

But that is many years away for Americans, and it is not my purpose to speculate in this book where we will be in 1990. Instead I hope to enlighten the ordinary investor as to how to stay afloat during the next few years of inevitable growing inflation.

Two Secrets to Profit During Inflation

There are two secrets to financial success in inflationary periods. They are:

(1) Buy equity—things that will go up in value as the dollar loses its buying power.
(2) Use borrowed money.

Secret #1: Buy Equity

During inflation, we have seen that paper investments, such as bonds, mortgages and insurance, lose their value because they don't go up in pace with inflation. We must therefore buy real objects—equity—which will rise in value. Where is the most *profit* to be made?

It is true that all real objects go up in price as the dollar goes down in value, but for investment purposes it is easy to eliminate most things. For example, it doesn't matter if butter is going to double in price over the next year. Obviously, we are not going to fill our homes with butter; because of storage and resale problems, the butter will all have gone bad long before any profit is possible. Similarly, we should not invest in anything which has a large discrepancy between the bidding and asking price. The buyer should be able to resell his purchase immediately at almost the same price. That is why it would be foolish to go to a jewelry store and buy expensive rings as a hedge against inflation. It may be true that those rings will move up 25% in price this next year because of inflation, but the purchaser has probably paid a 60% markup to the retailer.

The two problems of storage and net value eliminate most objects as protection from inflation. (It is a difficult concept for many people to accept—my wife still thinks she's protecting our assets from inflation every time she visits Saks Fifth Avenue.) What is left?

real estate
commodities
gold and other precious metals
some stocks
art and antiques
wine
old stamps, coins, books and rugs
memorabilia

The problem with all of these is that in themselves they cannot protect us from the ravages of inflation. The reason is simply this. Suppose you are forty years old, with a family and a good job bringing in $35,000 per year. Your life savings are $50,000. You invest your $50,000 in one of the above inflation-proof categories—for example, gold—and over the next five years, there is a 100% inflation and the gold goes up 100% in value to $100,000. Your standard of living, however, still falls. Although the gold has gone up enough to preserve the true value of your savings, this has done nothing about the falling value of your salary, which is not inflation-proof and which is most unlikely to go up as fast as the inflation. We must now understand the second secret.

Secret #2: Borrowed Money

Buying equity helps *keep up* with inflation, but the only way to *get ahead* of inflation is through the use of borrowed money. Let us take the same example. With the same assets and the same income, you now borrow an extra $50,000, using your own $50,000 as security, and buy $100,000 worth of gold. At the end of five years your $100,000 worth of gold is worth $200,000. After you have paid back the $50,000 you borrowed plus the interest, you have $125,000 left. You have crept ahead of inflation!

It only makes sense to borrow money if that money can be borrowed at less than the inflation rate, so obviously, one should not go to a loan shark or even a finance company. In fact, in only two fields of investment is it simple and cheap for the ordinary person to borrow long-term money: real estate and commodities. These are the two areas where huge profits will be made during inflation.

Is Equity Always the Thing to Buy?

There is one important point to remember about equity. Keep away from buying items retail which have a large spread between retail and wholesale prices. There is no profit to be made in buying a print at $100 retail, seeing it appreciate over five years to $200 retail, and then going back to the gallery where you bought it and being offered only its $100 wholesale value. I think that everyone understands that an object sold in any store is marked up anywhere from 50% to 100% and that only a fool would buy retail as an investment. Even though this appears obvious, it's surprising how many people forget this truism if the salesman is clever and the object is dressed up.

A perfect example is the sale of diamonds. Millions of dollars' worth of diamonds have been sold at inflated prices over the past five years to people who should know better. It seems obvious enough that when DeBeers marks raw diamonds up 20% to their wholesaler, and the wholesaler in turn marks them up another 30% to the distributor, and the distributor adds about a third on his sale to the jeweler and the jeweler adds 60% to 75% before the customer sees them, that it is going to take a pretty big move in diamond

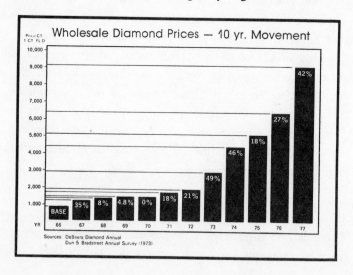

Wholesale Diamond Prices — 10 yr. Movement

PRICE CT
1 CT FL D

Sources: DeBeers Diamond Annual
Dun & Bradstreet Annual Survey (1973)

prices before the last man in the chain can sell at a profit. And yet very profitable high-pressure advertising and phone campaigns have succeeded in loading up thousands of simple people with quantities of diamonds as a spurious inflation hedge.

The pitch is remarkably simple. One firm reprinted a table (see facing page), showing price increases received by the De Beer diamond trust since 1966.

They then went on to tell potential customers:

In this age of financial uncertainty, it's comforting to know that one investment medium has continued to rise calmly through good times and bad. Since the 1930's the price of diamonds at the producer level has risen steadily, with no declines on any year-to-year basis. . . . Reasons we believe diamond prices will continue to rise:

(1) Supplies are dwindling while demand is growing.
(2) Diamond prices automatically adjust for inflation.
(3) Mining costs continue to rise.
(4) Political difficulties in southern Africa.

Jewelry demand for diamonds is currently consuming most everything that's being produced. Added to this, burgeoning investment demand provides additional upward impetus.

Well, maybe—but there is no question that an awful lot of promoters are making a pretty good living selling diamonds in just this way!

Don't buy diamonds. There is little chance of profit even if the price goes up. Twenty-five years ago my wife purchased a diamond bracelet for $1,500, and as it is now out of fashion and diamond prices are supposed to have gone up tenfold last year, she decided to sell. She discovered to her dismay that in the last ten years diamonds are cut in a different way and as her diamonds are "old cut" they are now worth $1,500! This is hardly the best inflation hedge.

Equity is useless as an inflation hedge unless you are buying at the *real* (wholesale) value. So forget about diamonds, old cars, prints or anything else if you are buying retail. But it is neither necessary to be in the business nor to be an expert to buy equity wholesale. More about that later.

Real Estate

Houses

Unquestionably, the first investment anyone should make in times of inflation is a house. It should be the most expensive home you can afford, with the biggest mortgage on which you can meet the payments.

There are many reasons to begin with a home:

(1) A house is easily bought with someone else's money, using a mortgage.

(2) Governments tend to avoid taxing profits on homes because there are so many voting homeowners.

(3) Mortgage interest is deductible from your income tax.

(4) You completely control the course of the investment, unlike a stock in which you are at the mercy of management.

(5) Housing prices tend to rise faster than the general inflation rate. As inflation progresses and rent control spreads, a shortage of rental accommodations

will develop, producing upward pressure on housing prices.

My secretary carried the maneuver out perfectly. Ann is forty-four, married, with two children. She and her husband, Russ, have worked all their lives, and in 1966 they took their life savings of $8,000 and bought a beautiful home for $46,500, paying for it with a government-guaranteed twenty-year 6¾% mortgage. Now, twelve years later, they still owe $30,000 on the mortgage, but because of inflation that $46,500 house is now worth about $250,000. Their equity is about $220,000. Note that it is not $46,500 that has grown to $220,000. All Ann and Russ put in was $8,000, and that $8,000 has grown to $220,000 *with no taxes* on the increased value. In no other way could an ordinary individual turn an $8,000 investment into $220,000 in twelve years.

This is just the beginning. As inflation speeds up, that $250,000 house could easily sell for a million dollars in six or seven years from now. This is a perfect example of how to profit from inflation.

When buying a house, don't worry about the interest rate on the mortgage so long as you can meet the payments. Interest rates always lag behind the inflation rate. More important, the mortgage rate remains constant throughout the life of the mortgage even though the inflation rate will continue to climb. Anyone today can repeat what Ann did twelve years ago. The only difference is that the numbers are higher. Today, first mortgages are available at 10% to 12%, and if you buy a house with such a mortgage, you are really not paying any true interest at all. The reason is that the buying power of the dollar is shrinking at the same rate, so that in effect the mortgage holder is lending you his money interest-free.

Furthermore, if one looks down the road five or ten years, the $50,000 or $100,000 mortgage you place now with today's dollars will be paid off, when it comes due, with vastly depreciated money. Today, $50,000 will buy an airplane. In ten years, I doubt it will buy a Cadillac. The result will be that the mortgage holder will have given a present of the house to you, the buyer.

I cannot stress it strongly enough. If you do not already own your own home, *buy it now!*

Rental Properties

Other types of real estate are a different matter. Probably the worst investment anyone could make today would be to buy an apartment house or duplex or any type of rental property. The reason is that governments come under intense pressure during inflation to "do something," and one very popular thing to do is to freeze rents. There are a hundred tenants for every landlord in the electorate, and it becomes irresistible for a politician to take this foolish but expedient move. I suspect that most politicians know that this is a mistake which inevitably results in a deterioration and shortage of housing. But try to explain that to an angry electorate squeezed by rising prices and falling true income. It is easier for the politician just to give in and let his successor worry about the problems that inevitably follow.

Much of the United States already has rent control and many areas are blighted as a result, but there is no doubt that as inflation gets worse, rent control will spread further. Those immediately hurt are the investors.

Barely a hundred miles from my home on the east side of Buffalo is a perfect example of the end results of rent control. As costs rose but rents remained frozen, housing maintenance gradually stopped and neighborhoods deteriorated. Finally, it no longer made financial sense to pay the taxes and one owner after another simply walked away from his investments. Today, a lot can be purchased in that part of Buffalo for $100. For $200, one can buy a lot with a house.

Don't buy rental income. It's a trap!

Farmland

Farms come in a special category of their own and represent an excellent investment today, second only to a family home. The farm represents a good investment for four reasons:

(1) Farmland goes up in price like everything else in inflationary times.

(2) Farms can be bought with someone else's money, using a mortgage.

(3) As cities grow, farmland gradually disappears and the remaining land becomes more valuable.

(4) Farms grow food, and while consumption of everything else will fall as inflation speeds up because of the general population's falling income, farmland has an extra value because everyone must eat.

If you buy a farm, do so with the largest, longest-running mortgage you can arrange and afford. Four years ago I purchased a 67-acre farm twenty miles outside of Toronto, paying $225,000, with $75,000 down and a

$150,000 mortgage. In the four years that mortgage has already run, the dollar has lost 30% of its buying power. The $150,000 now represents only $100,000 in terms of buying power.

There are land taxes to pay on farmland. Though the taxes tend to be low, it is advisable, wherever possible, to rent your land to a farmer. This will bring in enough income to at least cover the taxes.

Three warnings:

(1) There is always the danger of government initiating special taxes on profits made on land held for speculation. Ontario did this in 1974, effectively cracking the land market. Don't buy land anywhere if a future change towards this type of taxation is a possibility.

(2) Never buy any type of land that is far away from your home. There are innumerable sharpies selling inaccessible scrub in northern Ontario, described as lush vacation property to foolish New Yorkers, while Midwesterners are plagued by sellers of ocean-front Florida properties accessible only at low tide. If you are going to buy land, buy it within easy driving distance of your home.

(3) Real estate has the disadvantage of lack of liquidity. You can't get out in a hurry. A family home is an excellent inflation investment, but after that investment is made, you will probably do better looking elsewhere for your second venture.

Commodities

━━━━━━◆•◆━━━━━━

Commodities are anything grown from or found in the ground, including cocoa, coffee, orange juice, cattle, copper, gold, sugar, cotton, hogs, platinum and silver.

Dealing in commodities is gambling, and commodity trading cannot be indulged in unless you have money you can afford to lose. But commodities are one of the few places left where you have a chance of making a fortune from a few thousand dollars. The reason is the huge leverage. A trader puts down only 5% or 10% of the purchase price, and thus a 5% or 10% move either doubles his stake or wipes it out entirely.

Commodities respond to innumerable pressures, varying from the weather in Ghana to the supply of anchovies in Peru, from the state of health of Anwar Sadat to the success of rebels in Zaire. All the factors resulting in the price of any one commodity can never be known to any individual. This produces the excitement in commodity trading. No one knows for sure what will happen next, so the intelligent amateur has as much chance as the huge multinational traders.

The two requirements for a commodity to be traded must be:

(1) a fluctuating price
(2) storability

Commodity trading originally began as a way for farmers to sell their crop at a guaranteed price long before harvest time, and thereby guarantee themselves a profit. Also, it was a route whereby manufacturers could contract to buy their raw material in advance so as to be protected against future jumps in price. Over the years, speculators came in to the market to fill the gap when there was no buyer or seller, guaranteeing both farmer and manufacturer a profit and attempting in the process to make money for themselves. Only 20% succeed in making money, but it is fairly easy to be in that small group.

Commodities trade on an exchange just as do stocks, but there are important differences between commodities and stocks:

(1) Commodities have very low margins.
(2) Commodities have low commissions; about 1/10 of that on an equivalent amount of stock.
(3) Commodities must be paid for with cash in advance. If you buy a stock, you have five days to pay.
(4) When buying stock, you say, "Buy me 100 shares of AT & T." Commodities, however, trade in units and each unit varies with the commodity. Gold is 100 ounces, sugar is 112,000 pounds, cattle is 40,000 pounds. If you say, "Buy me three cattle," you are ordering the purchase of 120,000 pounds of cattle.

(5) Unlike stocks, each commodity has a daily "limit" to its price changes. Whereas a stock may plunge or soar on bad or good news, commodities are only allowed to move a certain amount each day. Cattle may not move up or down more than 1½¢ from the previous day's close (but remember that 1½¢ represents $600 per contract). These limit moves are great if the commodity is moving in the direction you have invested, but if it is going the other way, it can be very painful not to be able to sell out and take your loss.

Can the ordinary investor make money from commodities, and if so, how? There is a well-written and amusing book on investments (which was on last year's best-seller lists), terribly mistitled *The Only Investment Guide You'll Ever Need*,[1] that starts out by saying keep away from the commodity market because 80% of the players lose. The author finally works himself up to quote a study of 1,000 commodity traders in which not one made money. If all these suckers are losing, who is making that money? It's people like me.

In 1975 I made $4,400 net in the commodity market. In 1976 I made $48,200 and in 1977, $56,000. In 1978 I made $60,500. If anyone thinks I'm not telling the truth, you are welcome to inspect my trading account at the firm where I do my commodity trading: Friedberg & Co., 347 Bay Street, Toronto. I have achieved this by spending no more than fifteen minutes per day at commodities.

Nor am I some unique genius. In fact, my winnings are small potatoes compared to what some people have taken

[1] Andrew Tobias. Harcourt Brace Jovanovich, 1978.

out of the commodity market since inflation sped up three years ago. The reason my earnings are comparatively small is that I don't like to gamble. I limit my holdings to a maximum of twenty diversified contracts at any one time.

Well, what are the secrets?

First of all, let's go back to the inflation. What goes up in an inflation? Everything! And commodities represent everything. Whether you look at silver or cocoa, cattle or orange juice, almost all commodities are selling at higher prices than they were five years ago. It's true that they don't all go up at the same time or the same pace, and some are going down while others are going up. But the overall trend is up. The following rules are important for commodity trading:

Go with the trend. Buy commodities. Don't trade on the short side. Leave that to the professionals.

Be prepared to take many small losses, but maximize your profits. As soon as you are down 25% of your deposit, accept your loss and sell out. Let profits ride for the maximum time allowed in the contract. In 1973 I added up all my trades for the year and found that I had lost in 92 transactions and profited in only 12. However, I still showed a net profit of $14,000 for the year.

Be extremely careful of commodities that have had huge upward price surges. The inevitable correction may wipe you out before you get started. If you really feel like gambling, this is one time where selling something short can prove very profitable. My activity sheet for June 1977, which appears on the next page, illustrates these points.

In May 1977 coffee had a huge price surge going all the way from 50¢ to $3 following a freeze in Brazil. This $3 wholesale price translated into $6 coffee in the supermarkets and there was a lot of press and threats of consumer boycott. It was fairly obvious coffee prices were going to come back down. On May 20 I sold a coffee contract at $2.89. I was able to buy the coffee back on June 3 at $2.44, giving me a profit of $16,875. On the other hand, in the

DATE	BOUGHT	SOLD	COMMODITY	TRADE PRICE	AMOUNT	
					DEBIT	CREDIT
			BEGINNING LEDGER BAL.		4,728.14	
**** C O N F I R M A T I O N S F O L L O W ********************************						
77-06-03		1	77JUL COFFEE NY.	258.50		
77-06-03	1		78MAR COFFEE NY.	244.00		
77-06-03		1	77OCT PLATINUM	156.00		
77-06-03		1	77AUG GOLD-COMEX	142.20		
**** P U R C H A S E S A N D S A L E S F O L L O W *******************						
77-06-02	1		77JUL COFFEE NY.	263.50		
77-06-03		1	77JUL COFFEE NY.	258.50		
	1*	1*	P & S		1,875.00	
77-05-20		1	78MAR COFFEE NY.	289.00		
77-06-03	1		78MAR COFFEE NY.	244.00		
	1*	1*	P & S			16,875.00
77-05-03	1		77OCT PLATINUM	163.10		
77-06-03		1	77OCT PLATINUM	156.00		
	1*	1*	P & S		355.00	
77-05-26	1		77AUG GOLD-COMEX	144.20		
77-06-03		1	77AUG GOLD-COMEX	142.20		
	1*	1*	P & S		200.00	
			TOTAL GROSS P OR L			14,445.00
			TOTAL FEES & COMMISSIONS		302.00	
			NET P OR L *			14,143.00
			TOTAL ADJ			
			TOTAL NET CHANGE **			14,143.00
			NEW LEDGER BALANCE **			9,414.86

other three trades shown, one in coffee, one in platinum and one in gold, as soon as things began to go against me, I took my loss. I ended up losing in three out of four transactions, but still ended up with a net profit of $14,143 for the period.

Choose a reliable broker. It is amazing how many villains and dolts are in this field. Ask your would-be broker two questions: (1) Do you also personally handle stock trading? (2) Is your firm a member of the Chicago Mercantile Exchange or the Board of Trade? If he answers yes to the first or no to the second, try somewhere else. To do well, you need someone who specializes in this very tough field and you must take care not to link up with some fly-by-night firm that won't be there when pay-out time comes.

DATE	BOUGHT	SOLD	COMMODITY	TRADE PRICE	AMOUNT DEBIT	AMOUNT CREDIT
			BEGINNING LEDGER BAL.		702.00	
**** C O N F I R M A T I O N S F O L L O W ***						
77-02-24		1	77MAY OR. JUICE	72.75		
77-02-24		4	77JUL COTTON	76.50		
77-02-24		1	77MAY PLYWOOD	206.80		
**** P U R C H A S E S A N D S A L E S F O L L O W *******************************						
77-02-03	1		77JUL COTTON	74.00		
77-02-07	1		77JUL COTTON	75.20		
77-02-09	1		77JUL COTTON	76.25		
77-02-17	1		77JUL COTTON	77.50		
77-02-24		4	77JUL COTTON	76.50		
	4*	4*	P & S			1,525.00
77-02-03	1		77MAY PLYWOOD	194.70		
77-02-24		1	77MAY PLYWOOD	206.80		
	1*	1*	P & S			919.60
			TOTAL GROSS P OR L			2,444.60
			TOTAL FEES & COMMISSIONS		335.00	
			NET P OR L *			2,109.60
			TOTAL ADJ			
			TOTAL NET CHANGE **			2,109.60
			NEW LEDGER BALANCE **			1,407.60

Pyramiding is the way to make big profits from small investments. This is the means by which one uses one's profits to buy more of the same commodity as it moves higher, without putting in any more money. Above is an example of pyramiding.

Note that on February 3 I bought one cotton contract at 74, and a second on February 7 at 75.20, a third on February

9 at 76.25 and a fourth on February 17 at 77.50. If the cotton had continued to move higher, I would have bought more, but now, holding four contracts, I was running a large risk. Since I didn't want to take the chance of losing my entire profit, I sold out on the first sign of weakness on February 24, taking my $1,525 profit and steering on to other opportunities. This is the reasonable way to trade commodities and the way to make money.

It is essential to be well informed in this or any other investment. The basics are published daily in *The Wall Street Journal*, and many other financially oriented newspapers. A subscription to at least one of these is essential.

In addition, all commodity brokers distribute a market letter to their clients. The big firms, such as Merrill Lynch, sometimes send out a daily letter on *each* active commodity, but that is a little more information than the dabbler (like myself) really wants. One of the very best market letters that consistently has given good advice is that sent out gratis to its customers by my broker, Friedberg & Co. Friedberg is a small firm that accepts no new small clients, but it is possible to subscribe to the newsletter.

If you really want to be on top of things, you can rent a ticker tape from Translux Corporation for $125 per month (plus another $60 to the Chicago Mercantile Exchange or Currency Exchange), which will show you every trade simultaneously as it occurs. (Just for fun, I briefly put one in my office, but it diverted me too much from my medical practice.)

Try to go against the popular view. It is a good rule of thumb that once the price of a commodity reaches the front page of *The New York Times*, it's time to get out. When sugar hit 65¢, five years ago, the newspaper stories said that it was going to $1 per pound, and the same happened with coffee in 1977. Remember that the public is always wrong. In the case of gold, which hit all the front pages in the winter of 1979, the same danger as with sugar applies when you're only putting 5% down in the futures market. For those like myself, who believe much higher prices are coming for gold, it it much safer to buy bullion outright.

Before leaving commodities, I should point out that they can move up or down in price very, very rapidly and this quick action produces an excitement that some people just can't handle. The sort of person who can't sleep because he goes over and over in his mind what he should have done should never enter the commodities field.

If you don't have the time to give to commodity trading (unlike stocks, commodities must be watched very closely), but still want to put some of your money into this field, then consideration should be given to a *commodity fund*. These funds allow speculators with as little as $1,000 to put money into several commodities at once. The way it works is that a brokerage house will set up a million-dollar cash fund by selling 1,000 units at $1,000 each. This money is then invested in a broad cross section of commodities, so that each investor's $1,000 is divided up proportionally to the funds' total assets.

Some of these funds have done remarkably well. A recent analysis by *The Wall Street Journal* showed that one such fund grew from $30,000 in 1972 to over $700,000 in 1978. They don't all do well, however, and the *Journal* found one

Commodities

Symbols for the exchange on which each commodity is traded appear in brackets after the commodity, followed by the minimum contract size and the monetary units used in the table. Open interest is the number of contracts outstanding each month and not liquidated by delivery of the commodity or by an offsetting contract.

Exchanges: CBT—Chicago Board of Trade, KCBT—Kansas City Board of Trade. CME—Chicago Mercantile Exchange, NYCSE—New York Coffee and Sugar Exchange. NYC-TN—New York Cotton Exchange, NYM—New York Mercantile Exchange, NYCX—Commodity Exchange in New York, NYCO—New York Cocoa Exchange, IMM—International Monetary Market of the Chicago Mercantile Exchange.

METALS

—Season— High Low			High	Low	Close	Chg	Open Int.
PLATINUM (NYM)—50 troy oz.; $ per troy oz.							
428.50	174.30	Apr	417.90	408.00	408.70	- 2.30	4312
429.50	227.00	Jul	420.00	409.00	410.00	- 2.00	2703
430.00	230.00	Oct	422.00	413.00	412.00	- 1.50	848
428.00	238.00	Jan	424.00	410.00	414.00	- 1.00	921
430.00	278.80	Apr	426.10	420.00	415.30	- 0.80	300
430.00	315.40	Apr	424.00	424.00	416.80	- 0.50	264
422.00	409.50	Oct	426.00	426.00	418.70		2
Est. sales: 2,815; sales Wed. 2,962.							
Total open interest Wed. 9,351 off 4 from Tues.							
SILVER (CBT)—5,000 troy oz.; ¢ per troy oz.							
755.00	475.50	Feb	753.00	732.00	747.80	+13.80	0
764.50	493.00	Apr	760.50	738.00	757.00	+16.50	25796
772.20	499.00	Jun	768.80	746.00	765.00	+16.20	20347
779.90	504.50	Aug	777.10	755.00	773.10	+16.00	25606
787.60	527.00	Oct	785.50	762.50	781.30	+15.80	14476
795.40	534.00	Dec	793.90	771.00	788.00	+15.80	11962
803.50	541.00	Feb	801.90	783.50	798.20	+15.80	12364
811.60	573.50	Apr	810.90	804.00	806.70	+15.80	17876
819.70	588.00	Jun	819.50	812.50	815.30	+15.80	15464
828.10	600.00	Aug	828.00	820.50	824.10	+15.80	11705
837.30	637.00	Oct	837.30	829.00	833.10	+15.80	9279
846.50	656.00	Dec	846.50	832.00	842.30	+15.80	7349
855.10	670.20	Feb	854.50	847.00	851.70	+15.80	6554
864.70	698.00	Apr			861.30	+15.80	4776
874.60	713.00	Jun			871.10	+15.80	2996
884.80	737.00	Aug			881.10	+15.80	310
Sales: Wed. 13,043.							
Total open interest Wed. 187,309, up 203 from Tues.							
SILVER (NYCX)—5,000 troy oz.; ¢ per troy oz.							
751.00	592.50	Feb	747.00	747.00	741.20	+ 8.50	57
760.00	504.40	Mar	755.70	732.50	744.00	+ 8.90	16156
765.00	683.00	Apr	760.00	743.00	748.10	+ 7.90	66
769.00	500.50	May	764.60	743.00	752.20	+ 7.60	22672
777.00	501.50	Jul	773.10	750.50	760.50	+ 7.40	20173
785.00	502.50	Sep	781.70	761.29	768.90	+ 7.20	27432
796.50	558.50	Dec	794.00	773.00	781.10	+ 7.00	27257
799.50	569.00	Jan	795.00	778.40	785.30	+ 6.90	29396
808.90	582.00	Mar	804.00	786.80	793.60	+ 6.80	34692
818.40	610.50	May	809.00	795.20	801.90	+ 6.70	20382
826.90	642.50	Jul	820.00	802.00	810.20	+ 6.60	16965
828.00	672.50	Sep	812.00	812.00	818.60	+ 6.60	9184
Est. sales: 18,000; sales Wed. 19,457.							
Total open interest Wed. 224,508 off 1,199 from Tues.							
COPPER (NYCX)—25,000 lb.; ¢ per lb.							
86.70	69.30	Feb	86.70	84.70	86.70		0
87.40	60.80	Mar	86.20	84.20	86.20	+3.00	9125
87.40	79.45	Apr	86.50	86.05	86.65	+3.00	5
87.50	61.90	May	87.10	85.25	87.10	+3.00	18200
87.40	62.60	Jul	87.25	85.40	87.25	+3.00	8563
87.30	62.50	Sep	87.25	85.35	87.20	+2.95	5360
87.10	65.50	Dec	86.80	85.00	86.80	+2.80	7668
86.80	67.70	Jan	86.50	85.10	86.75	+2.75	1009
86.90	63.75	Mar	86.50	84.90	86.65	+2.65	11837
86.70	70.25	May	86.50	85.00	86.55	+2.55	1800
86.25	73.80	Jul	86.00	85.00	86.45	+2.50	829
86.20	75.55	Sep	86.00	84.40	86.35	+2.45	1380
86.50	82.10	Dec	86.50	84.80	86.20	+2.45	35
Est. sales: 13,000; sales Wed. 8,621.							
Total open interest Wed. 55,656 off 638 from Tues.							
GOLD (IMM)—100 troy oz.; $ per troy oz.							
285.90	167.90	Mar	251.20	245.70	246.20	- .50	13826
262.20	177.60	Jun	257.80	252.50	252.80	- 1.50	20764
269.00	181.00	Sep	264.90	259.50	259.90	- 2.00	12329
276.00	183.20	Dec	271.80	266.60	266.70	- 1.30	9206
283.50	210.50	Mar	278.70	273.00	273.40	- 1.40	6264

FOODS

—Season— High Low			High	Low	Close	Chg	Open Int.
COFFEE (NYCSE)—37,500 lb.; ¢ per lb.							
167.50	93.75	Mar	124.50	120.00	122.25	- 2.25	1812
163.50	94.00	May	123.80	119.41	123.46	+0.05	2092
163.13	92.00	Jul	125.50	119.63	124.36	+0.73	1743
158.75	90.00	Sep	125.50	120.62	124.81	+0.19	1361
137.00	92.50	Dec	124.50	119.28	124.16	+0.88	640
131.00	111.50	Mar	125.00	117.76	124.00	+2.25	220
131.00	116.00	May	124.75	117.51	123.92		123
Est. sales: 3,550; sales Wed. 654.							
Total open interest Wed. 7,991 off 229 from Tues.							
EGGS, Shell (CME)—22,500 doz.; ¢ per doz.							
59.00	51.40	Feb	58.30	57.50	57.50	.60	129
55.25	53.00	Mar	55.25	54.75	54.80	- .10	179
52.85	49.00	Apr	50.80	50.60	50.75	+ .15	201
52.60	48.70	May	50.35	50.10	50.10	+ .10	366
50.55	50.40	Jun	50.55	50.40	50.55	+ .25	1
58.65	56.50	Sep	58.00	57.65	58.00	+ .40	80
60.00	59.20	Dec	59.90	59.20	59.70	+ .20	17
Est. sales: 142; sales Wed. 162.							
Total open interest Wed. 973, up 12 from Tues.							
ORANGE JUICE (NYCTN)—15,000 lb.; ¢ per lb.							
129.50	80.15	Mar	114.80	113.90	114.75	+0.55	2758
129.50	80.15	May	116.60	115.80	116.15	+0.15	2266
129.50	80.25	Jul	118.25	117.10	117.55	-0.05	946
130.25	95.55	Sep	118.85	118.00	118.25	- 8.25	781
124.00	110.00	Nov	113.50	112.50	112.50	-0.75	43
118.00	89.50	Jan	109.00	108.15	108.45	- 0.30	78
118.30	93.50	Mar	109.00	107.95	108.45	- 0.30	61
113.75	107.25	May	108.90	108.70	108.20	- 0.55	214
Est. sales: 400; sales Wed. 637.							
Total open interest Wed. 8,902 up 26 from Tues.							
SUGAR, World (NYCSE)—112,000 lb.; ¢ per lb.							
11.03	6.55	Mar	8.57	8.39	8.48	+0.10	7501
11.23	6.70	May	9.00	8.77	8.86	+0.08	12214
10.99	6.87	Jul	9.27	9.06	9.15	+0.08	7646
10.30	7.05	Sep	9.46	9.28	9.36	+0.08	3488
10.38	7.15	Oct	9.59	9.38	9.47	+0.07	4098
10.95	9.32	Mar	10.20	10.04	10.13	+0.13	1537
10.41	9.69	May	10.41	10.27	10.33	+0.14	324
10.65	10.65	Jul	10.65	10.65	10.65		0
Est. sales: 8,825; sales Wed. 5,551.							
Total open interest Wed. 36,814 up 240 from Tues.							
SUGAR, Domestic (NYCSE)—112,000 lb.; ¢ per lb.							
16.50	14.20	Jul	15.52	15.52	15.65	- 0.15	883
Est. sales: 10; sales Wed. 83.							
MAINE POTATOES (NYM)—50,000 lbs.; ¢ per lb.							
6.78	4.86	Mar	6.02	5.94	6.02	+ .09	1614
7.19	5.14	Apr	6.23	6.17	6.23	+ .15	253
8.59	5.57	May	7.25	7.15	7.24	+ .12	11231
5.70	5.42	Nov	5.69	5.61	5.62	- .01	81
6.41	6.30	Mar	6.41	6.40	6.41		2
8.10	7.50	May	7.96	7.92	7.96	+ .13	46
Est. sales: 2,145; sales Wed. 2,105.							
Total open interest Wed. 13,227 up 222 from Tues.							
COCOA (NYCO)—30,000 lb.; ¢ per lb.							
163.00	111.50	Mar	157.25	153.75	157.45	+2.95	668
188.70	110.50	May	159.75	155.95	159.75	+3.25	1664
187.25	118.20	Jul	162.00	157.95	162.00	+3.50	1663
183.00	116.00	Sep	163.50	159.80	163.75	+3.25	1343
179.50	124.25	Dec	165.30	162.00	165.55	+3.15	1046
174.50	154.70	Mar	166.00	154.70	166.80		149
166.00	156.50	May	165.75	165.75	167.85		3
Est. sales: 1,088; sales Wed. 928.							
Total open interest Wed. 6,536 off 73 from Tues.							

FIBRES

FRIEDBERG'S
COMMODITY & CURRENCY COMMENTS

347 Bay Street, Toronto Ontario Canada M5H 2R7   Telephone: (416) 364-2700   Cable: Friedco Toronto   Telex: 06-23446

Real Interest Rates, at last ?   *Sept. 5th, 1979*

> " Over longer periods, I believe
> that it is essential to maintain
> positive real rates, at least before
> taxes "
>   H. Wallich,
>   Governors,
>   Federal Reserve Board

Not good enough, but definitely getting closer. For almost two years we have advocated a sharp and dramatic increase in U.S. interest rates as the only way out of the current impasse. At the time, Fed Funds were trading at a lowly 6.5% and the game of 'nickling and diming' increases was in its infancy. A full twenty-one months later, the Fed Funds stands at 11 3/8%, it is beginning to jump in 3/8 - 1/2 percentage points increments but it is still not sufficiently high to match genuine savings to genuine industrial needs. And now, an official of the Highest Order pronounces himself in favor of positive real rates. Not bad if so much blood had already not been spilled and not bad if he had left out the phrase ' at least before taxes. ' And not bad if he had serious company at the Washington Round Table.

But wait, just under his breath and in a paternalistic tone, he adds that " one reassuring factor is that the upward movement of BOND YIELDS (our emphasis) indicative of rising inflation expectation has been moderate. " That is no longer true. Over the past few weeks, long term rates have soared by almost 50 basis points.

Who is the Fed fooling ? Obviously, only some of the people and only some of the time. For in the past three months, the U.S. dollar has lost as much as 8% against leading European currencies in spite of intervention approaching $14 billion. From May and up to the end of July, the U.S. admits to having sold approximately $5.4 billion equivalent of DM and SF while up to the end of August foreign exchange reserves of Switzerland, West Germany, U.K. and Japan have collectively increased by $8.5 billion. If we assume that the U.S. spent another few billion dollars in August, we begin to realize the magnitude and desperation of the latest flight from the Dollar.

Like all things political, temporizing will be resorted to in the following months. The U.S. may move to increase once again its gold sales to raise necessary foreign exchange. Clearly, nothing less than two million ounces per month ($750 million) will have any significance. Since the objective will be to raise funds rather than to depress prices, the market will not be able to absorb, at least temporarily, more than three million ounces per month ($1 billion). This upper limit is suggested by the amount of total bids presented at the IMF and U.S. Treasuries.

The sale of Gold out of the U.S. Treasury has certain political advantages, namely : (a) does not require the Fed to raise interest rates to the ' choking point' in the midst of an apparent recession while risking White House and Congressional displeasure; (b) can be effected quickly and expeditiously, without congressional approval and potential leaks; (c) sooths the violently anti-gold faction in the U.S. Administration; (d) carries the most dramatic psychological force and (e) has a ready market and mechanism. The second expedient available, some sort of foreign exchange controls, is not easily administered, is unpopular, requires Congressional approval and is anathema to the likes of Paul Volker. As a result, it can be discounted, at least temporarily.

The above scenario calls for a specific trading strategy. Unfortunately, there is one and only one reponse that will fit this scenario and, should it not come to pass, the response could lead to financial ruination. We will, therefore, suggest an 'all-year-round' course of action in the full knowledge that it will not represent the optimum strategy.

1) Maintain a gold exposure but reduce it to an amount which, should a sudden $80/oz drop occur from any level, will not cause financial hardship,
2) Cover short positions in interest rates futures over the next few days.
3) Protect long positions in British Pounds via the sale of equivalent amounts of Japanese Yen.

commodity fund that dropped by 50% in just two years. *The Wall Street Journal* summed it up this way:

> The trading managers' past performance suggests that the systems will, at worst, lose investors' money a good deal slower than amateur speculators can lose it on their own, and at best, earn such speculators a great deal more money than they could earn themselves. That is a major reason why professional commodities management has become attractive to risk-tolerant investors in the past few years.

Thomson McKinnon and Shearson Hayden Stone are two New York firms offering such a service.

What bothers me most about such funds is that all of their investment decisions are made by a computer which attempts from past prices and trading to analyze what is going to happen. Such a method ignores all basic changes in supply and demand, current economic developments or even a sudden war that might drastically affect a commodity. I am very uneasy about computer trading. On the other hand, it is the only way to get into the commodity market with only $1,000 to start. (I should mention that the broker will ask his customer to sign a statement that he or she has a net worth of $50,000 or a yearly income over $20,000.)

Some of the smaller commodity firms have set up mutual funds in which they charge $2,500 per share, and many of these have been spectacularly successful. Here is the record as of the end of 1978 of the nine funds set up by one commodity broker from March 1976 to March 1978:

Name of Limited Partnership	Date Begun	Initial Capital	Date Ended	Capital at End of Sept. 78	% Change
Commtor I	Mar. 76	C$59,000	Mar. 77	C$173,374.45	+193.9
Commtor 1977	Mar. 77	159,000	Mar. 78	407,422.00	+156.2
Dealcom	Apr. 77	83,000	Apr. 78	96,198.35	+ 15.9
Zeifcom	May 77	75,000		140,080.96	+ 86.8
Olive	Oct. 77	160,000		233,312.39	+ 45.8
Marten	Oct. 77	127,000		175,866.83	+ 38.5
Nosegay	Dec. 77	78,000		212,499.85	+172.4
Commtor 1978	Feb. 78	350,000		502,111.91	+ 43.5
Stoat	Mar. 78	99,500		119,563.98	+ 20.2

(The particular company running the above funds does not solicit new clients and has asked me not to use its name.)

I really think the clever speculator is better off on his own. But if someone is nervous about starting, this is a relatively painless way to do it, although it is definitely a second choice. In my opinion, using a computer to pick an investment is just a modern version of charting.

The Mindless Guide to Investment

There is a widely held belief that if one carefully studies the past price movements of a commodity (or stock or currency), one will be able to predict its future price changes. Believers in this method carefully make charts of the daily (and sometimes hourly) prices and volumes at which their stock trades, and by studying the chart or picture this produces, they think that they can tell what is about to happen. The theory on which charting is based is this: No one can possibly know all the factors affecting the price changes of any security, but the market knows because all the individual buy-and-sell forces are exposed in the trading of that security. Furthermore, the pull in both directions will be clearly reflected in the way stock prices move up or down. Invariably, the same factors that produce a chart showing one picture will result in an upward price movement, while the factors that will end up in a downward price change show quite a different chart.

This theory of chart investments is nonsensical. It has always amazed me how many followers charts have. *No chart can foretell what price changes will occur tomorrow.* How could a chart know that a freeze is going to hit Brazil, thus causing the price of coffee to soar? I strongly urge my readers to ignore such a foolish nostrum.

And incidentally, there are other people, including stock advisers, who make their investments on the basis of the stars, their horoscope, hunches, hot tips or even what they see in the funnies. To all of these hopefuls I can only say good luck, for rationality is lost upon them.

Follow the above advice and you can take advantage of inflation instead of its taking advantage of you.

But remember this: the best trader following the most sensible rules will get clobbered occasionally in the commodity market. Don't enter this field unless you can afford to lose. For those seeking safety, there are far better places to put your money—such as gold bars or certificates.

Gold as an Investment

—◆••◆—

In 1966 in my first book, *Anyone Can Make a Million*, I wrote that gold that was then $35 per ounce would go up to at least $100 per ounce. In 1971, when gold had reached $80, I raised my prediction to $200. Now that gold has gone over $300, it is fairly obvious that much higher prices are coming: $500 within the year, $1,000 or even $2,000 within five years.

The logic is inescapable. Firstly, we should be aware that gold has not really gone up in price by a single penny, that is, a real penny. If you turn one ounce of gold into U.S. dollars, it will buy almost exactly the same amount of goods in the supermarket that one ounce of gold bought seven years back. No, gold has not gone up at all; it is the dollar that has gone down! And the reason the dollar has gone down in value is that there are twice as many of them as there were seven years ago. It's just as though you were slicing a pie. If you cut it into four pieces, they are all large and filling. But if you make eight slices out of that same pie, they are only half as big and half as filling. Yet in both cases they are a "slice," albeit representing very different amounts. It's just the same with the dollar. Today's dollar is called the same but it represents far less than the dollar of yesteryear.

So the question we must pose is not how high will gold go, but rather, how low will the dollar sink? There is no bottom, nor is there any point at which gold will stop rising. People tend to think there is some magic number, so they ask me, "What is gold worth?" when they should be asking, "What is gold worth today?" You wouldn't ask, "What is an apple worth?" Everyone understands that apples will cost more next year because of inflation. Gold is a commodity just like apples and it, too, will cost more next year.

Gold has one special quality that other commodities do not. It can be stored forever without deterioration, and because it is rare, a small amount represents a lot of value. And this is the reason that since the beginning of recorded history nations have used gold as an international medium of exchange. It is just a way to make trading easier. If there were no international trading medium, how could one nation exchange its wheat for another's oil, its cars for another's potatoes? Trade would slow to a crawl. Every transaction would have to be done by barter, with endless haggling. How much quicker when we know that fifty pounds of apples are worth one ounce of gold and so is one pair of shoes.

But since 1932 and John Maynard Keynes, gold is not used as a medium of exchange. Instead, nations pay for other nations' goods with IOUs which they call dollars or yen or marks, and those IOUs are worth more or worth less depending on how rapidly they are pumped out and how productive the economy is that prints them. The United States has issued far too many IOUs in relation to its assets, and as time goes by, those IOUs look less and less attractive to the people who are trading goods for them. The world needs some acceptable *constant* medium of exchange whose value does not depend on the policies of any government and which cannot become worthless if a government changes.

That medium need not be gold. It could be silver or wampum or sheepskins or platinum, but it must be indefinitely storeable without losing its qualities. Its total world supply must either remain constant or else grow at a predetermined rate. And it is these requirements that eliminate everything but gold. We can't use sheepskins because it would be too easy for someone to breed zillions of sheep (and anyway, they smell). We can't use wampum because it gradually deteriorates. We can't use silver because there is so much of it in the world that huge quantities would have to be transported with every intergovernmental fiscal transaction. We can't use platinum because there isn't enough of it. There is no magic in gold, but it *is* the only suitable medium of exchange.

And that brings into proper focus the comment emanating from the U.S. Department of the Treasury in August 1978 when that body increased its monthly gold sales from 300,000 ounces to 600,000 ounces. The spokesman said, "We're doing this to protect the U.S. dollar and to hurry up the demonetization of gold." What the Treasury was really doing was demonetizing the dollar, not the gold. It makes one wonder whether the gentlemen running that Department are villains or are just plain stupid.

Many nations in the past have gotten themselves into a financial bind through overspending and have attempted to solve that problem by abandoning gold and using paper money or IOUs. (The Romans substituted silver for gold and then brass for silver.) Invariably, the same result ensues. As the citizenry and other nations are flooded with paper money, there is a rush to get rid of this paper, which has no constant value, by buying hard goods, including gold. Some countries attempt to prevent this by forbidding their own nationals from owning gold. All that happens, in that case, is that other things, such as jewelry or antiques, are purchased in its place. And that in turn produces inflation, as more and more paper money is spent on an increasingly scarce supply of hard goods.

Inflations all end the same way—with a cataclysmic flood of worthless paper money which finally no one will accept. A new currency must then be created, and in order to restore confidence, it must be backed with something tangible, and you can be sure that something won't be sheepskins.

So back to gold. Certainly, it should be bought as an inflation hedge just like any other store of real value. But gold is an especially good buy because sooner or later the United States is going to have to return to it as a medium of exchange. The later that day comes, the higher the price that gold will bring—$400 per ounce sounds like a lot today; $2,500 per ounce is inevitable if present economic policies are continued. And that won't sound so ridiculous if you realize the $2,500 ounce of gold will buy only the same amount of goods it buys today. In my lifetime I've seen that very thing happen in Germany, in China, in Uruguay and in Chile. Why should America be immune from the simple law of economics that says that if you spend more than you earn, people won't want your IOUs?

Let me stress, however, that gold is not going to go straight up. Unquestionably, there will be intermediate dips which will eliminate the weak holders, and one of these will probably occur in the next few months when the United States raises its prime rate over 15%. This will produce a great flow of money into the United States, a consequent strengthening of the dollar and a temporary fall in the price of gold. But let me stress the word "temporary." High interest rates produce high unemployment and a recession, and high interest rates will have to be lowered before the 1980 elections if the Democrats are to have a chance. So we will see a new surge in gold and new high record prices in 1980.

If you are convinced that some of your assets should be in gold, there are several routes possible.

Gold Bars

Gold bars, which can be purchased from any international bank, are the cheapest way to buy gold. The bars are pure and cost only the quoted value of their gold content on the day of purchase. However, this is really not a very practical way to invest in gold: the bars are heavy; there is always the danger of their being stolen; they must be insured, and can only be resold at the same place you bought them (or else they must be reassayed). There are other problems. One veteran New York open-line radio host put his life savings into gold bars and ruptured himself while carrying them to a safety deposit vault! I don't recommend gold bars.

Gold Coins

Buying ancient gold coins has been a very profitable hobby in recent years, but here, too, many extraneous factors intrude, including the rarity of the coins, the popularity of that particular country's coins and the condition of the piece, so that actual gold content of the coin may not be the major factor in its value. In addition, coins of this type sell for anywhere from 25 to 1,000 times the value of their actual gold content. An upward move in the price of gold is not necessarily reflected in the value of the coins. Buying old coins is an excellent inflation hedge, but it is not the best way to invest in gold.

With one exception, modern gold coins are worse than ancient coins as an investment. Many nations now find it profitable to mint so-called proof gold coins at premium prices. A typical example was the $100 18-carat Olympic gold coin issued by Canada in 1976. The coins were sold at $140 each in a high-pressure international campaign and so many of them were produced that they had no chance of increasing in price because of rarity. They certainly couldn't go up in real value because their gold content was worth about $45. Three years after issue, with gold at an all-time high, these coins are selling at 10% *less* than the original price. All the lovely gold commemorative coins from various Caribbean countries that are advertised periodically fall into the same boat. They are a foolish investment, with no chance of profit.

The exception is the Krugerrand. This common one-ounce coin is issued by the South African government and is sold at the value of the gold that day plus a modest 6% premium. Krugerrand are about the size of a half dollar, can be easily stored in a safety deposit vault, are handily transportable, and can be bought or sold at any bank or currency exchange anywhere in the world at that day's gold value. And if you ever have to leave in a hurry (don't laugh—that's the reason they are so popular in Europe), a pocketful will sustain you for a long time. Everybody should have a few Krugerrand, but this is not the best place for large gold investments.

Gold Certificates

Certificates are one of the more sensible ways to purchase gold, and these can be bought from any international bank. Each certificate confirms that you the purchaser own x ounces of gold, but all that you actually take home with you is the certificate—you never actually see the gold. The advantage of this over bullion is that there is no risk of theft, no problem of storage and no requirement for insurance. The bank that sold you the certificate takes care of all those chores, and the cost is remarkably low—you pay only the actual value of the gold that day plus a small service charge, plus a nominal storage fee.

Gold Stocks

What about gold stocks? Gold stocks can be a very good investment, but many of these stocks will profit only the promoter behind them. These are the mining prospects, selling for pennies or for a few dollars, that are looking for an ore body or have a low-grade ore but are "waiting for higher prices." In other words, just because a company calls itself a gold mine doesn't make it so, and it's a pretty good rule of thumb to eliminate all of these by simply asking the size of the company's dividend. If it's producing gold and making money, it will be paying a dividend, and if there is no dividend, it is probably not a good buy.

One thing for sure, if a broker phones long distance to promote a gold stock, run for the hills. He's not doing it because he likes you. It's hard to believe, but thousands of people still lose millions of dollars this way every year.

There are, however, good investments in gold stocks. The first decision must be whether to buy gold stocks from Canada, the United States or South Africa.

Any dispassionate analysis shows that the South African companies are by far the best buy, both as to size of dividends and equity behind each dollar of share value. But I would suggest that despite this, these stocks should not be purchased because of the tremendous risk to capital. Everyone familiar with the troubles in Africa has seen the tide of black nationalism, moving south from central Africa into South Africa's border states. With Angola and Mozambique now ruled by men who have openly declared their hostile intentions towards South Africa, with Rhodesia going the same and South West Africa in turmoil, how long can it be till more violent disturbances reach South Africa? Once the troubles begin, one of the first places to be hit will be the gold mines, with their mass of underpaid black miners. A strike shutting down the mines would undoubtedly be followed by violence and turmoil.

This, of course, is the reason that South African stocks are so cheap. For those investors prepared to gamble that stability will be maintained in South Africa, there are some reasonably cheap stocks about. Do bear in mind that one reason for the very high dividends is that South African gold mines, unlike those in North America, pay out practically all of their income in the form of dividends. When the mine runs out of ore, they simply close down. This means that much of the dividends on which tax must be paid by the recipient is really a return of capital. That being said, the best investments in South African golds today are the following (in order of merit):

Name	Recent Price (Aug. 24/79)	Mine Life in Years	Est. 1980 Dividend with gold*			
			at $260 oz.		at $300 oz.	
			Div.	Yield	Div.	Yield
Harte-beestfontein	$31.00	20	$4.37	14%	$5.10	16.4%
Randfontein	53.00	25	8.05	15%	9.50	18.0%
Western Deep Levels	14.50	25	3.10	21.5%	4.00	27.0%
Southvaal	13.50	25	1.26	9%	1.70	12.5%

All of the above have a long life and a good chance of showing a profit for their holders, provided South Africa remains stable.

For those gamblers who think the price of gold is going to soar this year, there is no better vehicle than the marginal

South African mines with relatively little rich ore left. If their less-valuable ore becomes economic, the stock price could multiply many times. These investments include:

Name	Recent Price (Aug. 24/79)	Mine Life in Years	Est. 1980 Dividend with gold*			
			at $260 oz.		at $300 oz.	
			Div.	Yield	Div.	Yield
Stilfontein	$ 7.45	5	$1.26	17%	$1.70	23%
Welkom	6.00	5	1.38	23%	1.75	29%

In the short term, you will not be so well off in gold stocks on this continent. But the day will certainly come when your investment here will be of far greater comfort (and profit). And bear in mind that turmoil in South Africa's gold mines may destroy the market in those stocks but will also drastically push up the price of gold and that of stock in secure gold mines.

The three big gold companies in North America—Dome Mines, Campbell Red Lake and Homestake Mines—are all listed on the New York Stock Exchange and are all extremely sensitive to changes in the price of gold.

Dome Mines trades around $36 per share on the New York Exchange. In addition to its own gold mine in Ontario, it owns large oil holdings through Dome Petroleum, 56% of Campbell Red Lake, 60% of Sigma Mines, plus various holdings in Denison Mines, Canada Tungsten, Mattagami Lake, and Panarctic Oil. Dome is the conglomerate of the natural-resources field.

Dome has 12 million shares outstanding and earns about $3 per share, out of which 50¢ is paid in dividends. It is hard to evaluate Dome because of its huge oil holdings, but the company's net asset value is certainly equal to its trading price, and its potential is virtually unlimited. On the other hand, the company has already seen a dramatic run up in its stock price from 1973's $11.

Campbell Red Lake is not only a subsidiary of Dome; it is intimately involved in its parent company's affairs, holding interests in Dome Petroleum, Panarctic Oils and Denison Mines. The company is currently earning about $1 per share, out of which half is paid in dividends. It currently trades on the New York Exchange around $20.

Homestake is the richest gold mine in the United States, with diversified interests in lead, zinc, silver and uranium. In recent years the company has done well chiefly from its huge uranium holdings, while gold has meant less and less to its earnings. In the first half of 1978 Homestake earned only $2.7 million from gold out of a total earnings of about $12 million, so it no longer really rates as a "gold" investment.

On the other hand, the company has huge deposits of "wealth in the ground," chiefly uranium but also base metals. It is currently earning about $2.50 per share and pays out half of that in dividends. It trades on the New York Exchange around $34. It is not a bad inflation hedge, but doesn't compare to either Dome or Campbell.

For my money, I think Dome is the best all-around buy at present prices, but Campbell will move up relatively more in relation to a rise in the gold price. In my opinion, money can be made from any one of these three companies.

Gold on the Future Exchanges

Finally we come to the most desirable way to speculate in gold: by buying bullion on the future exchanges. Gold is listed on three exchanges: Chicago Mercantile, New York's Monetary and Winnipeg. The contracts traded in New

York and Chicago are for 100 ounces and those in Winnipeg are for 100 or 400 ounces. In Winnipeg, there is a slight advantage in commission, but the market is much thinner and therefore less liquid. Here are the trading results for one day. The volume in Winnipeg was only 24 contracts while 17,000 were traded in Chicago and 14,000 in New York.

```
GOLD  (CMX)-100 troy oz.; $ per troy oz.-s
Sept     209.10 209.10 206.90 205.90     -1.00     216.00 186.00
Oct      210.00 210.50 207.50 207.60     -1.00     218.00 152.00
Dec      213.00 213.50 210.30 210.60     -1.00     221.50 153.50
Feb79    216.00 216.00 213.50 213.80      -.90     224.90 161.80
Apr      219.80 219.80 216.90 217.10      -.80     228.00 163.00
June     223.00 223.00 220.10 220.50      -.70     231.30 164.80
Aug      224.20 224.80 224.20 223.90      -.60     234.80 176.80
Oct      229.70 229.70 229.70 227.30      -.60     238.20 183.40
Dec      232.70 233.10 231.20 230.80      -.60     241.80 187.60
Feb80    236.80 236.80 236.80 234.30      -.60     245.00 190.50
Apr      ....  ....  .... 237.80          -.60     248.20 212.00
June     243.80 243.80 240.80 241.30      -.60     252.50 231.30
     Est.  sales 16,500; sales Wed.:  17,291 contracts.
GOLD  (IMM)-100 troy oz.; $ per troy oz.
Sept     207.50 209.00 205.20 205.40-.20  -1.3to1.5  216.50 146.20
Dec      212.70 213.50 210.10 210.30-.60  -1.3to1.0  221.50 152.50
Mar79    218.00 218.40 214.80 215.30-.50  -1.1to.90  226.60 167.90
June     223.30 223.30 220.10 220.50-.40  -.90to1.00231.80 177.60
Sept     277.60 228.50 225.60 225.70      -.80      236.50 181.00
Dec      232.90 233.50 230.60 230.60     -1.20      241.30 188.20
Mar80    238.20 238.50 238.00 238.00     +1.00      246.50 210.50
June     ....  ....  .... 244.00s        +1.40      252.00 233.00
     Est.  sales 11,258; sales Wed.:  13,916 contracts.
GOLD  (WPG)-400 troy oz.;/ $ per troy oz.
Oct      209.90 210.20 207.70 207.70     -1.10      217.70 155.50
Jan79    214.40 214.70 212.00 212.00b    -1.00      222.60 169.90
Apr      219.00 219.00 216.80 216.80a    -1.30      228.00 181.00
July     ....  ....  .... 221.80a        -.10       232.00 197.40
Oct      ....  ....  .... 228.50a        -1.00      237.50 219.40
     Est. sales 30; sales Wed.: 24 contracts.
```

Gold Listing from The Globe and Mail

Because of the much greater volume, the difference between the bid and ask is smaller on the two U.S. exchanges, and so it's easier both to buy and to sell. Therefore, it is wiser to use Chicago or New York rather than Winnipeg.

Note that the gold sells by delivery date, and the further away the delivery chosen, the higher the price. This is only partially because the market expects a rise in the price of gold. The difference between the futures price for October 1978 of $207.60 and October 1979 of $227.30 also represents the interest on the invested money plus storage charges for one year.

The advantages of buying gold in this way are:

(1) No risk of theft. The buyer never actually takes delivery of the gold.
(2) No insurance costs.
(3) Low margin. The down payment on one contract of 100 ounces worth about $40,000 is only $2,500. This provides big leverage.
(4) Price changes depend only on the value of the gold, eliminating extraneous factors such as size of ore body or labor unrest.
(5) Large profits can be made very quickly through the use of pyramiding, which involves purchasing more gold contracts with the profits from earlier purchases without putting up further capital. This is gambling. My trade sheet for July 1978 (which appears on the next page) is an example of this type of pyramiding.

Note that on July 20 I set the base of the pyramid by buying seven December gold contracts, five at $195 and two at $196.30. I then built my pyramid by buying two more contracts the next day at $200.10 and $201.40, one more on July 24 at $201.90, four more on July 28 at $208.20 and $209 and the final one on July 31 at $210. Thus, with the pyramid complete, I had a $13,000 profit with gold at $209.80, and one week later, when December gold reached $220 (and I began to sell), my fifteen contracts showed a paper profit of $28,000 from an initial investment of only $17,500, and all this in three weeks!

DATE	BOUGHT	SOLD	COMMODITY	TRADE PRICE	SETTLEMENT PRICE	DEBIT	CREDIT
			BEGINNING LEDGER BALANCE				973.91
78-07-03	1	1	78SEP CAN.DOLLAR				40.00
78-07-05	2	2	78SEP CAN.DOLLAR				
78-07-06	4	4	78SEP CAN.DOLLAR			710.00	
78-07-26	4	4	78SEP GER.MARK			270.00	
78-07-28	2	2	78SEP GER.MARK				1,347.50
**** O P	E N	T R A	J E S F O L L O W ****				792.50
78-07-05	1		78SEP GER.MARK	49.29	49.61		
78-07-05	1		78SEP GER.MARK	49.40	49.61		400.00
78-07-07	1		78SEP GER.MARK	49.16	49.61		262.50
78-07-10	1		78SEP GER.MARK	49.53	49.61		562.50
78-07-10	1		78SEP GER.MARK	49.60	49.61		100.00
78-07-24	1		78SEP GER.MARK	49.41	49.61		12.50
	6						250.00
78-07-20	5		78DEC GOLD-COMEX	195.00	209.80		1,587.50*
78-07-20	2		78DEC GOLD-COMEX	196.30	209.80		7,400.00
78-07-21	1		78DEC GOLD-COMEX	200.10	209.80		2,700.00
78-07-21	1		78DEC GOLD-COMEX	201.40	209.80		970.00
78-07-24	1		78DEC GOLD-COMEX	201.90	209.80		840.00
78-07-28	3		78DEC GOLD-COMEX	208.20	209.80		790.00
78-07-28	1		78DEC GOLD-COMEX	209.00	209.80		480.00
78-07-31	1		78DEC GOLD-COMEX	210.00	209.80	20.00	80.00
	15						13,240.00*
					OPEN TRADE EQUITY		14,827.50

Of course, gold does fluctuate and I was lucky in my timing, but the overall trend is up because of inflation. Provided you don't get in over your head and can ride out short-term reversals, you will make money. If your capital is limited, it is advisable to protect gold positions with stops $3 or $4 below the current price. This limits any loss and you can always reinstate your position when the downward surge stops. This is what I did in May of 1977, buying gold at $144 and seeing it move up $5 and then down to what

I had originally paid. I had approached my stopping point and I sold out, but I bought it back again a few days later (at $145) and waited for the next upward move.

If you don't wish to gamble on margin buy the most distantly traded month. It doesn't make sense to put up all your cash at the broker because no interest is paid. This is one place where government or other interest-bearing certificates make sense. Put down the minimum margin and place the balance in short-term government notes, which can be left with the broker. It's just as though you had bought the gold outright but without the nuisance of looking after it.

And as an extra, you will make a bonus on your interest-bearing certificate because the markup on the gold is actually less than current interest charges. The chairman of Mocatta Metals Corporation, Dr. Henry G. Jarecki, explained this on August 19, 1979, to *The New York Times*:

A 100-ounce gold futures contract maturing in September 1980 on the Commodity Exchange in New York is selling for $330 an ounce, or $33,000 in all. Usually an individual would have to put up 10 percent, or about $3,000, as an initial cash margin to buy that contract. The price of a September 1979 Comex gold contract is now about $300 an ounce, or $30,000. The contract price includes such costs as financing, storage, insurance and related carrying charges calculated for the life of the contract, in this case one year.

But the carrying charges built into the futures prices are far below the cost of money today. In effect, the one-year cost to the investor works out to 8.5% on an annual basis. If one went to a bank to borrow $30,000 for one year for the purchase of gold bullion and got it, the interest cost would be $3,600 at a prime rate of 12%. Far more likely he would pay 15% or more.

So here you have your gold plus a little extra. It's not painful to lend out money at 11% or 12% today when your cost is only 8.5%.

It is all common sense. Whether you believe in gold in some mystical way, as do so many of the "gold bugs," or whether you just acknowledge that everything is going up in price—in either case gold is one of the most practical ways to protect capital.

I personally do it all the sensible ways. I own Campbell Red Lake stock, I buy gold futures and I even have a few Krugerrand. I haven't lost on any of them in the past. I expect to continue to profit in the future.

Making Money
by Selling
U.S. Dollars

———— ·•·• ————

Suppose you already own your own home and don't want to gamble in commodities or speculate with gold. Where can you invest your money where the capital is safe and where there is some real return on it? In other words, what is today's equivalent of the government bond of preinflationary days?

U.S. dollars have been falling steadily in value for the past ten years as more and more of them have been printed, but this is not true of other currencies from countries with non-inflationary policies, such as Switzerland, Japan, West Germany and Chile. The German mark still buys almost as much hard goods as it did ten years ago and the Swiss franc buys even more. Too bad our savings are not in one of those foreign currencies.

Take care, the last time I made that suggestion, a lady in the Midwest actually went out and converted all her life savings into Swiss francs—actual bank notes—which she took home with her. The idea was fine and she did make money, but the method was all wrong. If you do convert your dollars into another currency, it's smart to do it in a way that will give a return. Ten years ago anyone could simply have opened a savings account in a foreign bank and happily drawn interest while the dollar sagged, but so many people did that and there was such a huge inflow of U.S. currency into the hard-currency countries that their own economies became threatened. Other countries responded by restricting foreign deposits, and Switzerland went so far as to charge foreigners interest on their accounts instead of paying it. At first this was nominal, but when that didn't stop the inflow they imposed a penalty interest rate of 10% every ninety days!

Buying Foreign Currency Bonds

The smartest way to hold foreign currency is through Samurai bonds, bonds issued by non-Japanese governments or non-Japanese corporations but payable in Japanese yen in both principal and interest. These bonds have grown rapidly in popularity. In 1970 only $25 million worth were issued, while in 1977 $1.2 billion were issued. The final figure for 1978 was over $5 billion. The Japanese government has welcomed such bonds because of their desire to lower their balance-of-payments surplus, and foreign borrowers have made the trek to Japan because of the low interest rates. (I think they are crazy, for when pay-off time comes they may well find that they saved 2% in interest and lost 100% in a capital loss.) But from the buyer's point of view, Samurai bonds are a perfect vehicle with which to change weakening dollars into hard currency and to draw interest on that foreign currency.

An amazing variety of countries have used Samurai bonds to raise money, and the interest rate will vary with the credit worthiness of the issuer. Here is a list of current Samurai bonds:

Name of Issue	Coupon	Date of Maturity	Amount Issue (billion yen)
No. 1 World Bank	7.75%	July 10, 1981	11
Asian Development Bank no. 3	7.3	May 6, 1982	10
Australia no. 1	6.9	July 25, 1982	10
Province of Quebec no. 1	6.9	September 28, 1984	10
Brazil no. 1	8.25	November 12, 1985	10
Finland no. 1	9.25	July 17, 1987	10
New Zealand no. 1	9.0	November 4, 1987	10
European Investment Bank no. 1	8.9	August 3, 1988	10
Denmark no. 1	9.0	November 30, 1988	10
Province of Manitoba no. 1	8.6	February 28, 1987	12
Banque Française du Commerce Exterieur	7.6	July 13, 1989	20
Ireland no. 1	7.2	August 5, 1989	16
Inter-American Development Bank	6.8	September 29, 1989	15
Province of New Brunswick	7.0	September 30, 1989	12
Spain no. 1	7.0	October 29, 1987	15
Venezuela no. 1	6.8	December 15, 1989	20
Singapore no. 2	6.7	December 27, 1987	15
Province of Manitoba no. 2	6.7	January 30, 1990	15
Korea Development Bank	6.7	January 29, 1988	10
City of Oslo	6.6	February 27, 1990	15
Finland no. 3	6.7	February 26, 1988	25
Societe Nationale des Chemins de Fer Française (SNCF)	6.6	March 10, 1990	20
Philippines	6.7	March 30, 1988	15
Malaysia	6.5	April 11, 1988	15
Argentina	6.4	April 17, 1986	15
Norway	5.7	April 18, 1983	25
RENFE (Spanish National R.R.)	6.5	April 25, 1990	16
Sweden	6.3	April 25, 1990	40
Province of Quebec no. 2	6.4	May 23, 1990	30
Republic of Venezuela no. 2	6.4	May 30, 1990	40
Eurofima	6.3	May 26, 1990	10
BNDE	6.5	May 30, 1988	16
City of Stockholm	6.4	May 15, 1990	10
Industria!ization Fund of Finland	6.4	June 18, 1990	5

Sellers of Samurai bonds have already taken a fearful beating. Take as a horrible example the province of Manitoba's issue in February 1977 of 12-billion-yen worth of these bonds. At the then conversion of 226 yen to the Canadian dollar, the hapless treasurer of that province ended up receiving about $5 million and assumed that he was to pay 8.6% interest per year. But because of the fall of the Canadian dollar since then, one dollar today buys only 165 yen, so the Province of Manitoba, which thought it was paying low interest, is actually now paying almost 11% annual interest on its loan. Worse, if they were to pay that loan off today, it would cost them well over $7 million. Who knows how high the final bill will be by the time those bonds come due in 1987?

But it is not my purpose here to criticize stupid governments or politicians. Rather, it is to show how to take advantage of their stupidity, and that is by *buying* Samurai bonds. If you had been one of the lucky buyers of a Manitoba bond in 1977, you would have already gained 40% on your money in interest and capital gain! Of course, one should use a certain amount of discrimination. I'm not at all sure that the government of Korea will be around in 1988 to pay off their bonds and so I wouldn't buy them. But I have no doubts that Manitoba, Denmark and Oslo are good for theirs. Buyers of these bonds receive the full interest return, for unlike other securities, the Japanese government does not hold back any withholding tax.

Where does one buy such bonds? Unlike most other securities, in the case of Samurai bonds there are more would-be buyers than there are new Samurai bonds available, so most dealers are not anxious to sell to small investors. Two companies that will handle small purchases are Daiwa Securities in New York City and Nomura Securities in Toronto's Commerce Court.

Samurai bonds are not the only way to invest safely in foreign currencies. Many bonds are issued denominated in German marks or Swiss francs. For example, last spring the World Bank announced that it was issuing six-year notes paying 5.75% and ten-year notes paying 6% denominated in German marks to a maximum of 400,000,000 marks. They are available through any international broker.

When buying German, Swiss or Japanese bonds, it is wise to purchase new issues rather than outstanding bonds already trading at a premium because with the new issue you avoid paying commission.

Trading in Foreign Currency

So much for the person playing it safe. How should a speculator gamble in foreign currency? Once again we must look to the Chicago Currency Exchange, where the currencies of France, Mexico, England, Canada, Germany and Japan are traded against the U.S. dollar. A list of quotes and trades appears every day in *The Wall Street Journal*:

```
MEXICAN PESO (IMM)—1 million pesos; $ per peso
.04349 .03030 Sep        .04370 .04367 .04370        217
.04265 .03035 Dec        .04298 .04270 .04298 + 17    611
.04150 .03450 Mar        .04194 .04173 .04195 + 27    707
    Sales: Fri. 116.
    Total open interest Fri. 2,269, off 13 from Thurs.
    Net change quoted in points, 1 point equals $0.0001.
SWISS FRANC (IMM)—125,000 francs; $ per franc
.6395 .4515 Sep          .6182 .6130 .6165 + 44       750
.6530 .4580 Dec          .6313 .6254 .6278 + 21       2989
.6620 .4625 Mar          .6435 .6394 .6412 + 32       731
    Sales: Fri. 1,831.
    Total open interest Fri. 4,842, up 526 from Thurs.
    Net change quoted in points, 1 point equals $0.0001.
BRITISH POUND (IMM)—25,000 pounds; $ per pound
1.9890 1.6430 Sep        1.9450 1.9295 1.9430 + 120    1007
1.9870 1.6750 Dec        1.9310 1.9130 1.9275 + 115    3844
1.9860 1.7530 Mar        1.9185 1.8955 1.9115 + 120    348
    Sales: Fri. 579.
    Total open interest Fri. 3,268, up 103 from Thurs.
    Net change quoted in points, 1 point equals $0.0001.
CANADIAN DOLLAR (IMM)
100,000 dollars; $ per Canadian dollar
.9168 .8608 Sep          .8615 .8587 .8593 - 29        357
.9300 .8575 Dec          .8605 .8575 .8587 - 18        3668
.9030 .8655 Mar          .8600 .8556 .8560 - 30        234
    Sales: Fri. 579.
    Total open interest Fri. 3,268, up 103 from Thurs.
    Net change quoted in points, 1 point equals $0.0001.
WEST GERMAN MARK (IMM)
125,000 marks; $ per mark
.5203 .4540 Sep          .5015 .4972 .5013 + 33        1111
.5280 .4570 Dec          .5084 .5042 .5081 + 36        3534
.5358 .4687 Mar          .5215 .5160 .5215 + 39        749
    Sales: Thurs. 2,222.
    Total open interest Fri. 5,501, off 309 from Thurs.
    Net change quoted in points, 1 point equals $0.0001.
JAPANESE YEN (IMM)—12.5 million yen; ¢ per yen
.005507 .004225 Sep      .005213 .005192 .005210 + 35  877
.005602 .004445 Dec      .005315 .005273 .005298 + 42  3001
.005682 .004485 Mar      .005385 .005345 .005368 + 45  681
    Sales: Fri. 2,653.
    Total open interest Fri. 4,568, up 657 from Thurs.
    Net change quoted in points, 1 point equals $0.000001.
FRENCH FRANC (IMM)—250,000 francs; ¢ per franc
$c.23860 .19280 Sep          .22850                    75
.23780 .19400 Dec        .22850 .22850 .22850 - 25     80
    Sales: Fri. 0.
    Total open interest Fri. 0, off 0 from Thurs.
    Net change quoted in points, 1 point equals $0.00001.
```

The essential point to remember is that the long-term trends of the yen, the Swiss franc and the German mark are upwards, while U.S. dollars are in the course of a long-term deterioration.

In currency trading, margin is even lower than with commodities, usually running about 2.5%. Thus each Canadian dollar contract, for instance, represents 100,000 Canadian dollars but requires only a $2,500 down payment. This results in rapid profits and losses. For example, if you had sold one Canadian dollar contract the day after Renée Lévesque was elected Premier of Quebec, you would have seen your $2,500 grow to $12,500 within one year without pyramiding and to over $200,000 with pyramiding. This was because the dollar went straight down. Pyramiding is dangerous, however, because currencies usually have zigs and zags in their moves, and with such a tiny down payment you should leave yourself some room.

An example of how to sell a collapsing currency on its way down appears on the following page.

And don't let anyone tell you that selling U.S. dollars is unpatriotic or that speculation is the cause of the collapse. It just isn't true. Every speculator ends up buying and selling exactly the same number of dollars. If I sell short one million dollars today, I must buy back exactly the same amount of dollars before my contract comes due in six months. My final total effect on the level of the dollar is zero. The real cause of our currency's collapse is the terrible overspending by our politicians. Being human, they will blame anyone before admitting their own culpability. Thus I was amazed one day when sitting in Ontario's legislature to be suddenly singled out by the leader of the opposition party, who said that the real cause of high food prices was people like me because I traded in the commodity futures market!

DATE	BOUGHT	SOLD	COMMODITY	TRADE PRICE	SETTLEMENT PRICE	DEBIT	CREDIT
			BEGINNING LEDGER BALANCE			2,751.78	
**** O P	E N	T R A	D E S F O L L O W ****				
77-09-29		2	78MAR CAN.DOLLAR	93.00	90.18		5,640.00
77-10-03		1	78MAR CAN.DOLLAR	92.51	90.18		2,330.00
77-10-03		1	78MAR CAN.DOLLAR	92.62	90.18		2,440.00
77-10-03		1	78MAR CAN.DOLLAR	92.65	90.18		2,470.00
77-10-04		1	78MAR CAN.DOLLAR	92.20	90.18		2,020.00
77-10-04		1	78MAR CAN.DOLLAR	92.30	90.18		2,120.00
77-10-05		1	78MAR CAN.DOLLAR	92.06	90.18		1,880.00
77-10-05		1	78MAR CAN.DOLLAR	92.24	90.18		2,060.00
77-10-06		1	78MAR CAN.DOLLAR	91.75	90.18		1,570.00
77-10-06		1	78MAR CAN.DOLLAR	91.85	90.18		1,670.00
77-10-11		1	78MAR CAN.DOLLAR	91.63	90.18		1,450.00
77-10-11		1	78MAR CAN.DOLLAR	91.66	90.18		1,480.00
77-10-12		1	78MAR CAN.DOLLAR	91.48	90.18		1,300.00
77-10-13		1	78MAR CAN.DOLLAR	90.85	90.18		670.00
77-10-24		1	78MAR CAN.DOLLAR	89.61	90.18	570.00	
		16					28,530.00*
MARGIN-	REQ				OPEN TRADE EQUITY		28,530.00
INIT	MAINT						
40000	32000						

Perhaps not surprisingly, the accusation came from a gentleman who had advocated huge welfare and farm-support programs and whose party has led my country to its present state of near-insolvency. I didn't take the accusation too seriously—nor did anyone else—but such attacks make great newspaper headlines. And it doesn't really matter whether they are true or not. If they reach the press, enough people will believe them to make it worthwhile. So my advice is to ignore such nonsense. But if you have a thin skin, keep your trading to yourself.

The mechanics of trading currencies is exactly the same as that of trading eggs or gold. But the one great advantage is that there are far fewer factors affecting any price change. Unlike ordinary commodities, once a currency enters a trend, it is rare indeed for it to reverse itself. Thus, the Canadian dollar has been steadily working its way lower since November 1976, while the U.S. dollar has been in its downtrend now for many years. Traders who have steadily sold these currencies short have made money year after year. But not day after day. Even the Canadian dollar in its precipitous collapse of 1977 and 1978 had brief periods of steadiness and occasionally even moved up fractionally.

So this brings me to the one danger in currency trading. Even long-term trends are interrupted occasionally, and on only 2½% margin this can be disastrous. So keep a reserve and don't put all your eggs in this one basket. Also, this is one place where it's sensible to protect yourself with stops no more than 1% from the current market.

But despite this one caveat, currency trading is the easiest and quickest place to make big money today. The easiest and safest are Samurai or German bonds.

The essential question is: What is the dollar worth? The first answer is that it is probably worth just about what it is now trading at, *but* that next year it will be worth less. Both Canada and the United States are committed to deficit financing, which means pumping out more and more dollars. Six years ago a U.S. dollar would buy four German marks. Today it will buy two German marks, and by 1984 it will probably buy only one mark. Ten years from now it may take four U.S. dollars to buy one mark. Similarly with the Canadian dollar. Canada's leading economists said it wouldn't break 90¢ U.S. As I write, it is just above 84¢. So long as we continue to follow our present economic policies, the Canadian dollar will continue to deteriorate. I can easily see 80¢ in 1980 and 50¢ in 1983. And people who don't protect themselves against an improvident government are improvident investors.

Offshore Funds: How to Make Money & Minimize Taxes

The only serious drawback to investing in Samurai bonds is the fact that the government grabs a big hunk of the interest paid on these bonds. Since no one likes to pay unnecessary income tax, a strategy has been developed which avoids paying this tax. It is very simple and is done through an offshore fund. *It is perfectly legal.*

A large number of these funds have been set up by reputable foreign brokers, and a few by some not so reputable (more about that later), which will take money from U.S. investors and with it buy hard currency bonds or stocks. The reason no income tax is payable is that the funds do not pay interest to the investor; instead, the interest is allowed to accumulate. This defers the tax indefinitely, and when the investor finally sells his shares, he pays tax only at the much lower capital-gains rate.

In addition, there are ways that an investor can actually draw this interest but still only pay tax at the lower capital-gains rate. This is done by selling 10% of the holdings every year. Suppose an investor puts $50,000 into an offshore fund earning 10% a year. Normally, he would pay income tax on the $5,000 interest, leaving him with $2,500 if he was in the 50% bracket. Instead, he draws no interest and in its place he sells 10% of his stock at the end of each year, giving him $5,500 in hand. He pays only a capital-gains tax on this, leaving him $3,900. Neat, is it not?

The only real problem with offshore funds is that they

are not under the scrutiny of the SEC, so great care must be taken in choosing a reliable fund. Martonmere Securities of Toronto has prepared a list of offshore funds with well-established sponsorshop and financing, through which a prudent investor can place his money in hard currencies. The following pages provide a selection from their choices.

1. Fixed Income Funds

Rentak Fonds

THE FUND INVESTS IN:
The Rentak Fonds invests in German government bonds, high-quality corporate bonds, and other types of bonds.

CURRENCY DENOMINATION:
German mark (DM)

INCORPORATION AND LOCATION:
The Rentak Fonds is incorporated under the laws of the West German Republic and maintains its offices in Munich, West Germany.

SPONSORS AND ADVISERS:

Investment Adviser	Münchner Kapitalanlage AG, Munich
Banker and Custodian	Allgemeine Deutsche Credit-Anstalt
Registrar and Transfer Agent	Allegemeine Deutsche Credit-Anstalt (ADCA) Frankfurt
Auditors	Treuarbeit AG, Munich

INTEREST:
The rate of interest on German government bonds and high-quality corporate bonds varies depending on German rates. At time of writing, it is around 6%.

DIVIDENDS AND APPROPRIATION OF PROFITS:
Interest and all other income are reinvested rather than paid out; hence no dividends are paid.

TAX POSITION:
There is no witholding tax paid or withheld on interest on any of the debt securities in which the fund invests, and the fund is not subject to capital-gains tax.

FUND SIZE:
At the end of September 1977, the total assets of the fund were DM 33.6 million, equal to $15 million (Cdn.)

RECORD (FINANCIAL YEAR DECEMBER 31):

	Accumulated Value DM	% Gain	Accumulated Value $ Cdn.	% Gain
May 1973	50.00	—	17.05	—
Dec. 1973	53.80	7.6	19.82	16.25
Dec. 1974	58.50	7.4	24.08	21.40
Dec. 1975	67.74	15.8	26.28	9.14
Dec. 1976	75.38	11.3	32.24	22.65
Sept. 1977	82.65	9.6	38.39	19.00
Average Annual Compound Gain		12.3		20.6

RE-INRENTA

THE FUND INVESTS IN:
The policy of Re-Inrenta is to invest primarily in German and high-quality corporate and other types of bonds which are not subject to withholding tax. As at September 30, 1977, the fund was entirely invested in German-mark securities.

CURRENCY DENOMINATION:
German mark (DM).

INCORPORATION AND LOCATION:
The fund is incorporated under the laws of the West German Republic and maintains its offices in Frankfurt/Main.

SPONSORS AND ADVISERS:

Investment Adviser	Deutsche Gesellschaft für Wertpapiersparen m.b.H. (DWS), Frankfurt/Main
Banker and Custodian	Deutsche Bank AG, Frankfurt/Main
Registrar and Transfer Agent	Deusche Bank AG, Frankfurt/Main
Auditors	Treuverkehr AG, Frankfurt/Main

INTEREST:
See Rentak Fonds.

TAX POSITION:
There is no withholding tax paid or withheld on interest on any of the debt securities in which the fund invests. The fund is not subject to capital-gains tax.

FUND SIZE:
At the end of September 1977, total assets were DM 45.9 million or $21.6 million (Cdn.) approximately.

VALUATION AND REDEMPTION:
The fund is valued every day and published in leading European financial newspapers. Payment is made as soon as possible after the next valuation date.

RECORD (FINANCIAL YEAR DECEMBER 31):

	Accumulated Value DM	*% Gain*	*Accumulated Value $ Cdn.*	*% Gain*
Dec. 1972	50.00	—	15.55	—
Dec. 1973	51.70	3.4	19.05	22.5
Dec. 1974	56.20	8.7	23.14	21.5
Dec. 1975	64.30	14.4	24.95	7.8
Dec. 1976	72.00	12.0	30.80	23.4
Sept. 1977	79.30	10.1	36.90	19.8
Average Annual Compound Gain		10.2		20.0

OBLIGESTION

THE FUND INVESTS IN:

Obligestion invests in fixed-income securities internationally, with the main emphasis (67% of portfolio) in Swiss-franc denominated bonds.

CURRENCY DENOMINATION:

Swiss franc (Sfr.)

INCORPORATION AND LOCATION:

The fund was incorporated in May 1973 under Swiss law and maintains its offices in Geneva, Switzerland.

SPONSORS AND ADVISERS:

Investment Adviser	Banque de Paris et des Pays-Bas (Suisse) S.A., Geneva
Banker and Custodian	Banque de Paris et des Pays-Bas (Suisse) S.A., Geneva
Custodians outside Switzerland	Brown Brothers Harriman, New York
	Deutsche Bank, Frankfurt/Main
	Euroclear, Bruxelles

	Banque de Paris et des Pays-Bas, Paris
Auditors	Fiduciaire OFOR S.A.

INTEREST:

The average rate of interest on the company's portfolio varies depending on the level of interest rates prevailing in the countries in which the fund invests. As of September 30, 1977, it approximated 6%.

DIVIDEND AND APPROPRIATION OF PROFITS:

The net income of the fund is distributed annually.

TAX POSITION:

As far as possible, the fund invests in debt issues which are exempt from withholding tax. Furthermore, it arranges for at least 80% of its income to be derived from foreign sources, so that distribution to unit holders domiciled outside of Switzerland can take place without declaration of the federal withholding tax.

FUND SIZE:

On September 30, 1977, total assets were Sfr. 31.5 million, equal to $14.5 million (Cdn.).

VALUATION AND REDEMPTION:

The fund is valued each week. The Banque de Paris et des Pays Bas makes an over-the-counter market. Payments are made in two days.

RECORD (FINANCIAL YEAR SEPTEMBER 30):

	Accumulated Value Sfr.	*% Gain (% Loss)*	*Distribution in Sfr.*	*Accumulated Value $ Cdn.*	*% Gain (% Loss)*
May 1973	100.00	—	—	31.55	—
Sept. 1974	89.15	(10.9)	9.40	29.33	(7.0)
Sept. 1975	99.60	11.7	6.60	37.75	28.7
Sept. 1976	113.30	13.7	6.95	45.03	19.3
Sept. 1977	124.65	10.0	—	57.21	27.0
Average Annual Compound Gain		5.2			14.7

EUROPE OBLIGATIONS

THE FUND INVESTS IN:

Europe Obligations invests in high-quality government, provincial and corporate bonds which are, with a few exceptions, not subject to withholding taxes. Basically, these are international bonds denominated in various hard currencies. The objective of the fund is capital appreciation and income.

CURRENCY DENOMINATION:

Luxembourg franc (F. Lux.)

INCORPORATION AND LOCATION:

The fund was incorporated in March 1973 under Luxembourg law and maintains its offices in Luxembourg.

SPONSORS AND ADVISERS:

Investment Advisers   Caisse des Depots et Consignations, Banque de L'Union Europeenne, Caisse d'Epargne de l'Etat du Grand Duche de Luxembourg, Banque Generale du Phenix, US

	Trust Paris, Deutsche Girozentrale — Deutsche Kommunalbank.
Bankers	Caisse des Depots et Consignations, Banque de l'Union Europeenne, Caisse d'Epargne de l'Etat du Grand Duche de Luxembourg.
Registrar Custodian and Transfer Agent	Caisse d'Epargne de l'Etat du Grand Duche de Luxembourg

INTEREST:

The rate of interest paid on the fund depends on the level of interest rates prevailing in the countries in which the fund invests. As of September 30, 1977, the rate of return was approximately 7½% free of tax. At the shareholder's option, interest may be kept in the fund and compounded rather than paid out.

TAX POSITION:

Except for shareholders domiciled or resident in Luxembourg, there is, at present, no Luxembourg income tax or capital-gains tax payable by the fund or its shareholders.

FUND SIZE:

As of September 30, 1977, the total net asset of Europe Obligations were close to F. Lux. 200 million or $6.1 million (Cdn.).

VALUATION AND REDEMPTION:

The fund is valued every day and the net asset value per share is published in the *International Herald Tribune*. Payments for shares being redeemed are made in Luxembourg francs as soon as possible after valuation day.

RECORD:

	Accumulated Value F. Lux	% Gain (% Loss)	Total Value $ Cdn.	% Gain (% Loss)
April 1973	1,000.0	—	24.87	—
Dec. 1973	1,011.8	1.18	24.40	(1.89)
Dec. 1974	938.6	(7.23)	25.71	5.37
Dec. 1975	1,163.4	23.95	29.91	16.34
Dec. 1976	1,224.3	5.23	34.39	14.98
Sept. 1977	1,337.6	9.25	40.16	16.78
Average Annual Compound Gain		6.8		11.5

2. Equity Funds
Henderson Baring Japan Fund
(originally established as Henderson BSM Japan Fund)

THE FUND INVESTS IN:

The Trust Deed empowers the Manager to invest the trust property in Japanese securities and, in respect of not more than 15% of the value of the trust property at the time of investment, in securities issued by entities of certain other countries in the Far East, including Hong Kong, Singapore, the Philippines and Malaysia. It is the main policy of the Manager to seek long-term capital growth, although there is some small current yield. The Manager expects that the portfolio will ordinarily be invested in equities or securities convertible into equities. The portfolio may, however, be retained in cash and/or invested in bonds or other types of security. At September 30, 1977, all investments in the fund were in Japan.

CURRENCY DENOMINATION:
U.S. dollar ($U.S.)

ESTABLISHMENT:

Established as a unit trust under the laws of the Bahamas. The offices of the management company are in Hong Kong.

SPONSORS AND ADVISERS:

Manager	Henderson Baring Fund Managers Ltd., Hong Kong
Investment Adviser	Henderson Baring Management Ltd., Hong Kong
Trustee and Registrar	Bank of New Providence Ltd., Nassau, Bahamas, a subsidiary of Chemical Bank, New York
Custodians	The Sanwa Bank Limited, Tokyo The Hong Kong and Shanghai Banking Corp., Hong Kong
Legal Advisers	Slaughter and May, London and Hong Kong, and Isaacs Johnson & Co., Nassau, Bahamas
Auditors	Deloitte, Haskins & Sells, Nassau, Bahamas

TAX POSITION:

Since under existing Bahamas legislation, the fund is not subject to tax in the Bahamas, there is no tax payable in respect of gains realized by the fund on the sale or redemption of securities forming part of its portfolio. Distributions by the fund to unit holders are not subject to the deduction of withholding taxes in the Bahamas.

In Japan, there is no capital-gains tax, but there is a with-holding tax on dividends of 20%.

DISTRIBUTION:

The net income of the fund after deduction of allowable fees and expenses will normally be distributed to unit holders in dollars on May 15 and November 15 in each year. The first distribution for the year ended March 1977 was paid in April 1977.

VALUATION AND REDEMPTION:

The net asset value per unit of the fund is calculated twice a month. Payments for the units realized will be made in dollars within seven days after valuation day.

SUBSCRIPTION:

Subscriptions can be sent to the offices in Nassau, or to Henderson Administration, London, or to Baring Sanwa Multinational Ltd., Hong Kong (for onward transmission to Nassau). Both the minimum holding and the minimum addition to an existing holding by a unit holder is 50 units.

FUND SIZE:

As of September 30, 1977, the total net assets of the fund amounted to $10.3 million U.S. The fund's assets were 92% in equities and convertible bonds and 8% in cash.

RECORD:

	Accumulated Value $ U.S.	% Gain
March 1976	9.90	—
March 1977	12.94	30.7
Sept. 30, 1977	13.34	3.0

Fleming Japan Fund S.A.

THE FUND INVESTS IN:
The Fleming Japan Fund invests in Japanese equities. Its main investment objective is capital appreciation, and consequently, only a small dividend is paid out.

CURRENCY DENOMINATION:
U.S. dollar ($U.S.)

INCORPORATION:
The fund is incorporated under the laws of the Grand Duchy of Luxembourg.

SPONSORS AND ADVISERS:

Investment Adviser	Robert Fleming Investment Management Ltd., London
Banker and Custodian	Kredietbank S.A., Luxembourgeoise, Luxembourg
Registrar and Transfer Agent	Kredeitbank S.A., Luxembourgeoise, Luxembourg
Auditors	Wimmey, Murray, Ernst & Ernst

TAX POSITION:
Under present legislation, the fund's investment income from sources within Japan is subject to normal Japanese withholding tax. No capital-gains tax is payable by the fund on the realized capital appreciation of its assets. There is at present no Luxembourg income tax, withholding tax, capital-gains tax, estate or inheritance tax payable by the fund or its shareholders, except for shareholders domiciled, resident or having a permanent establishment in Luxem-

bourg. The fund is subject in Luxembourg to annual duty of 0.16% on the aggregate value of the outstanding shares of the fund. This value is calculated by reference to the Luxembourg Stock Exchange value of the shares during the preceding year. The fund is also liable to a contribution duty of 1% of the nominal value and premium on new issue of capital.

DISTRIBUTION POLICY:
Since the main objective of the fund is capital appreciation, it pays out only a small dividend.

VALUATION AND REDEMPTION:
The fund is valued weekly and the net asset value per share is published in *The Financial Times*. The shares are quoted on the Luxembourg Stock Exchange. Payment is made in U.S. dollars within the first 15 business days in which certificates are received by the fund.

FUND SIZE:
Total net assets at September 30, 1977, were $40 million (U.S.).

RECORD (FINANCIAL YEAR DECEMBER 31):

	Accumulated Value $ U.S.	% Gain (% Loss)	Distribution U.S. $	Accumulated Value $ U.S.	% Gain (% Loss)
Dec. 1971	15.17	—	—	15.17	—
June 1972	22.70	49.6	—	22.47	48.1
June 1973	17.35	(23.5)	0.090	17.28	(23.0)
June 1974	19.01	10.0	0.100	18.47	6.9
June 1975	21.42	12.7	0.140	21.91	18.0
June 1976	29.45	37.4	0.125	28.53	30.0
Sept. 1977	36.76	24.8	0.150	39.44	38.2
Average Annual Compound Gain		16.6			18.1

Concentra

THE FUND INVESTS IN:
Concentra invests in the shares of leading German companies. Its objective is long-term growth.

CURRENCY DENOMINATION:
German mark (DM)

INCORPORATION:
Concentra is incorporated under the laws of the West German Republic, and as a German mutual fund, is subject to the provisions of the German Investment Institutions Act. Its offices are in Frankfurt/Main.

SPONSORS AND ADVISERS:

Investment Adviser	Deutscher Investment Trust, Frankfurt/Main
Banker and Custodian	Dresdner Bank AG, Frankfurt/Main
Registrar and Transfer Agent	Dresdner Bank AG, Frankfurt/Main
Auditors	Treuhand-Vereinigung AG, Frankfurt/Main

TAX POSITION:
With the exception of corporation tax levied on dividends cashed by the fund, Concentra is exempt from all German taxes on income and property. German tax at source (Kapitalertragsteuer) is deducted neither from the fund's income nor from distributions.

VALUATION AND REDEMPTION:
The fund is valued every day and redemptions are made as soon as possible after valuation day. The units are listed on the German stock exchange.

FUND SIZE:

Total net assets on September 30, 1977, were DM 1,828 million or $840 million (Cdn.).

DIVIDENDS:

Concentra makes a yearly dividend distribution. For the fiscal year ended December 1976, out of total income per unit of DM 2.43, DM 1.20 was paid out and DM 1.23 was reinvested.

RECORD (FINANCIAL YEAR DECEMBER 31):

	Net Asset Value Per Unit Including Reinvestment of Distribution DM	% Gain (% Loss)	Distribution in DM	Net Asset Value Per Unit Including Reinvestment of Distribution $ Cdn.	% Gain (% Loss)
Dec. 1971	25.52	—	2.60	7.83	—
Dec. 1972	27.93	9.4	2.60	8.69	11.0
Dec. 1973	23.46	(16.0)	1.80	8.64	(0.6)
Dec. 1974	24.20	3.2	1.80	9.96	15.3
Dec. 1975	33.18	37.1	1.80	12.87	29.2
Dec. 1976	31.42	(5.3)	1.20	13.44	4.4
Sept. 1977	34.19	8.8	—	15.91	18.4
Average Annual Compound Gain		5.2			13.1

In summation, offshore funds are a highly sophisticated way of protecting capital by putting it in German marks, Swiss francs or Japanese yen, while simultaneously earning a reasonable income and, most extraordinarily, shielding that income from taxation. It's a great way to invest!

What About the
Stock Market?

Unlike the bond market (yecch) or the gold market (hurrah), there is no simple answer as to the future of common stocks. The reason is that because every stock represents ownership in a different company and every company faces different prospects during inflation, great discrimination is necessary.

It is fairly certain that utilities and other regulated companies will do badly in inflationary times. This is because as inflation and costs of doing business speed up, companies in this class have great difficulty in getting approval of rate increases quickly enough. Let me give one example from my own experience. When I was a legislator and inflation was running at about 6% per year, the local telephone company was faced with tremendous cost increases for both labor and materials such as copper, which had sold five years earlier at 40¢ per pound and which had now reached 80¢. Yet when the company applied for a 6% rate increase, dozens of well-meaning or popularity-seeking politicians presented briefs to the regulatory body as to why the raise should not be allowed (I weep with embarrassment—I was one of them), giving as their major reason the company's profits of millions of dollars per year. Last year I made the mistake of trying to reason with one of my former colleagues on this subject, but his response was right to the point, "To hell with return on capital and the same for the telephone company. There aren't any votes there."

Ultimately the company did get its raise, but the hearing, with all its briefs, resulted in a delay of six months between initial application and final approval. It didn't matter too much in 1970, but today costs would be so much higher in six months that a new application for a raise would be needed immediately. *In inflationary times, telephone stocks and power companies are a losing proposition.*

Service companies are just about as bad because their costs go up with the inflationary rate, but there is great resistance to raising service prices at the retail level. To take the simplest example, if the cost of a haircut is raised from $3 to $6, people get fewer haircuts (or cut their own). *Service companies are a bad investment in inflationary times.*

High-profile manufacturing companies are not much better. General Motors sets its price once a year, and has great difficulty in putting on hefty rises even then because of governmental pressure "to set an example." I wouldn't buy manufacturing stocks today.

Well, what stocks are worth buying? Only those that are inflation-proof and there aren't many of those. An inflation-proof stock is one that has "wealth in the ground," that is, not susceptible to government control. All "wealth in the ground" stocks are not inflation-proof, and this has been illustrated only too well in the United States in recent years. When world oil and gas prices surged in the mid-seventies, the federal government passed laws forcing the oil companies to sell their gas at prices far below the world market price. Voters applauded, and since there are far more of them than there are shareholders in Standard Oil, the government continued this policy. This was very short-sighted because any such artificial ceiling automatically reduces exploration.

So the only stocks worth buying today are those with "wealth in the ground" where there is no advantage to the government to jump in. That includes companies exporting their product (like the Canadian lumber companies), for no politician cares what prices are like in another country, companies producing something that is not considered a necessity (gold mines fall into this category) and companies holding big land spreads. These few stocks will move up in price at least as fast as the dollar loses its buying power, but they are the only group that will do so. Other individual stocks may do well, for example, a drug company making a major discovery or a manufacturing concern that is attractive as a takeover, but in general most stocks are not inflation-protected and should be avoided.

One extra dividend to "wealth in the ground" stocks is that they are a special attraction for takeover offers from nervous holders of cash seeking good investment. Asbestos Corporation was an excellent example of this type of investment. In the fall of 1977 the company had enormous deposits of asbestos in Quebec, had a net asset value of $65 per share, paid an 8% dividend and was trading at $23. I bought a total of 5,000 shares for myself, and attempted to persuade all my friends it was the buy of the age. I even wrote an article in October 1977 for the *Magazine of Wall Street* saying that it was a sure way to make money. I never did find anyone else who bought the stock, but only thirty days later the Quebec government made an offer to buy out the company. I made a killing! Here is one of my trade slips.

As for preferred stocks, none should ever be bought. In a preferred, the holder sacrifices participation in profits in return for a steady dividend, and that can become a terrible mistake for the holder as interest rates rise. *Forget preferred stocks.* If you have any, sell them.

New stock issues are coming back as a way of making easy money. In the late sixties a lot of money was made by the purchase and immediate sale of new stocks that came out and went to an immediate premium. The new-issue market collapsed in 1969 largely because so many companies went public with few real assets and with grossly overpriced stocks, but in 1978 there was a definite rebirth in the new-issue market. It is likely new issues will have another boom as the inflation speeds up. Here is an example of a new stock issue.

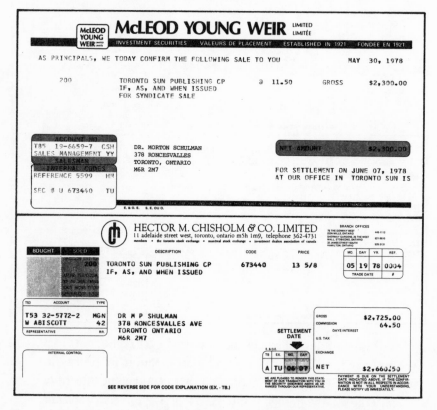

There are two advantages to hot new issues. One is the chance to make a profit without any risk and the second is the fact that your capital is not tied up for more than one or

two days. Also, there is no commission paid on the purchase. These issues are much sought after and are hard to
get, so brokers usually dole them out to their good customers. If your broker hasn't cut you in on such goodies,
you should try another broker.

One final warning about stock investment. You are
running the risk of being taken by traders who take illegal
advantage of insider information. In 1978 Robert Bleiberg
wrote in *Barrons* that "illegal trading on inside information
is running riot up and down Wall Street." This was followed by an article by Nicholas von Hoffman in *The
Washington Post* on August 19, 1978, in which he said:

> This law is broken so often that *The Wall Street Journal*
> reported there is circumstantial evidence that there was
> illegal insider traffic in the stocks of 27 out of 30 U.S.
> companies subject to merger offers in April and May of
> this year alone.
>
> Many also don't buy because Wall Street has gone
> out of its way to merchandise itself as an international
> casino. Along with the executives of many of the com-
> panies whose stock Wall Street sells, brokers have pushed
> the idea of buying as a gamble on future price rises so
> long and so loud, they have convinced the world that
> owning stock is a leisure-time activity, an entertainment
> diversion for money you don't really need and can
> afford to lose.
>
> Stockholders see their money sunk into bombas-
> tically designed, horrendously expensive headquarters
> buildings and into fancy private jets. They look at their
> shrunken, misshapened investments, their flat dividend
> checks and listen to the screaming about ending tax
> deductions on the three-martini lunch. They know the

government only picks up half the tab for those drinks and they also know who picks up the rest, so they sell out and buy bonds or real estate or antique toys—anything that will hold its value.

To which I can only add—Amen.

Stock Advisory Services

There is an amazing amount of information, misinformation, advice and misadvice churned out from Wall Street. Much of it is in the form of analysis of different stocks put out by the research departments of the larger brokerage houses, and most of this is reasonably accurate if not of particular value. The problem with these is that by the time the customer actually receives the information sheet, it has already gone through far too many hands. Even if the information was of real value, too many people have already acted upon it.

As for advisory services, forget them. The people running them are often unqualified and/or unprincipled, and an amazing number of "puff" stocks have been pushed up and out using this route. There are some honest and good services, but the average investor finds it impossible to tell the good from the bad. I write for one service which I think is pretty good, but it is basically a course on investing, not a tip sheet.

In 1977 I had the great pleasure of interviewing one Dr. H. S., a famous stock adviser who says he charges his investors $2,500 per year for his advice, which he assured my audience was worth many times that figure. I then confronted Dr. S. with his market letter from exactly one year earlier in which his commodity recommendations had all gone the wrong way; the ones he said to buy had gone down and the ones he suggested selling had gone up! Needless to say, Dr. S. was not pleased with me.

And Dr. S. is no worse in his recommendations than dozens of others. What it boils down to is that this is a sucker's game. Save your money and don't subscribe.

Higher Interest Rates Can Be Profitable

When I wrote the first draft of this book the prime rate was 10½%. As I revise these lines the prime rate is up to 15%, and the bleats of rage from borrowers can be heard all over the United States. Higher prime rates mean higher interest on mortgages and higher costs for every loan in the land, and one furious writer called it "loan-sharking made legal."

In actual fact, interest rates are still far too low and must go higher. The reason is quite simple. If the inflation rate is 15%, anyone lending money out at anything less than 15% is actually taking a real loss in buying power every time he makes a loan. *Interest rates must rise to a figure higher than the inflation rate or it makes no sense to make loans.*

What this means is that as the inflation speeds up, interest rates must continue to rise. There may be temporary interruptions for political reasons, for example, just prior to a federal election it makes good political sense to force interest rates down in order to gain some temporary popularity. But any such action can only be carried out by speeding up the printing presses, with a consequent acceleration of the inflation, and therefore, such an action can be only temporary. The inevitable final result is higher inflation accompanied by an even higher interest rate than would have eventuated without government action.

Looking down the road, I can easily see a 20% prime rate within the next year or two, and this gives astute investors an opportunity to make money—not by lending out money, for that is a sucker's game, but through the medium of Ginnie Maes.

Gambling with Ginnie Maes

GNMAs (Government National Mortgage Association Certificates, or Ginnie Maes as they are more affectionately called), are twelve-year U.S. mortgages, which in today's financial climate offer an opportunity to make a great deal of money. Normally, mortgages are sold on an individual property, but GNMAs represent a pool of tens of thousands of mortgages divided into $100,000 pieces.

Each GNMA theoretically yields 8% per annum, but in practice the true yield will vary with prevailing interest rates. As mortgage interest rates go up, the value of GNMAs goes down. If interest rates rise over 8%, the price at which each GNMA can be sold will fall below $100,000 until the $8,000 interest paid each year comes in line with current mortgage rates. Suppose mortgages are currently 8% and a GNMA is sold for $100,000. Six months later suppose that interest rates have risen to 9% and the GNMA holder wishes to sell. The GNMA will sell at a figure yielding 9%, that is, the face value is still $100,000 but it will bring on the market only about $90,000 ($8,000 interest on a $90,000 investment is approximately 9%.).

Unlike ordinary mortgages, GNMAs trade on an exchange and their current price is listed every day in the financial newspapers. Here is a sample listing:

GNMA 8% (CBT)—$100,000 prncpl; pts., 32nds of 100%								
	Open	High	Low	Settle	Chg	Close	Yield Chg	Open Interest
Dec	.....	.....	.....	.....	....	.....	....	336
Mar	87-31	88-01	87-26	87-27	+ 3	9.758	− .015	6,486
June	88-01	88-04	87-29	87-30	+ 3	9.743	− .015	7,124
Sept	88-09	88-13	88-05	88-05	+ 2	9.708	− .010	6,012
Dec	88-14	88-15	88-09	88-10	+ 3	9.682	− :016	6,809
Mar80	88-13	88-13	88-05	88-05	+ 3	9.708	− .015	7,058
June	88-07	88-07	88-01	88-01	+ 1	9.728	− .005	8,638
Sept	88-05	88-05	87-30	87-30	+ 1	9.743	− .005	8,492
Dec	88-01	88-02	87-27	87-27	....	9.758	....	6,192
Mar81	87-30	87-30	87-21	87-21	− 2	9.789	+ .011	3,688
June	87-26	87-26	87-19	87-19	....	9.799	....	1,680
Sept	.....	.....	.....	87-16	....	9.814	....	73
Est vol 4,542; vol Thu 5,245; open int 62,588, +446.								

GNMA Certificates Listing from The Wall Street Journal

Note that the price is quoted in terms of $1, not $100,000. This is just for brevity. GNMAs fluctuate by thirty-seconds of a point, and each $\frac{1}{32}$ represents $\frac{1}{32}$ of $1,000, or about $31. A move from 100 to 101 is really a move from $100,000 to $101,000 and represents a difference of $1,000. Note that the September 1979 GNMAs closed at 88\frac{5}{32}$, up $\frac{2}{32}$ on the day—that is, each owner saw his investment rise in value by $62 that day. Note also that GNMAs trade by months. The month named is the month that the mortgage actually begins. You will see that in the subsequent months, the price is lower. This is because it is widely expected that interest rates will rise in the future; thus, GNMAs will fall in price.

How can one make money on mortgages? Certainly not by buying them. As I pointed out earlier, mortgages are a terrible investment in inflationary times. Profits lie in *selling* mortgages. But how does one sell something one does not own? It works something like selling a stock short.

Look again at the sample quotation listing. The June GNMAs closed that day at 87.30, which means that someone bought a June GNMA for $87,900 and someone sold at the same price. But a June GNMA is a mortgage beginning the following June. Not until June does delivery take place or does the mortgage begin to bear interest. What the two people have traded is the intention to carry out a transaction next June, and because the mortgage is not yet in existence, the money need not be put up until June—ten months later. Instead, each party deposits the sum of $2,000 with his broker as a guarantee. Anytime before next June the buyer may sell his GNMA or the seller may buy back a similar GNMA, unloading the transaction except for whatever profit or loss may have ensued.

Because only $2,000 is being put down on an $87,000 transaction (a little over 2%), the leverage is very high. If that GNMA moves to 89 from 87, the buyer's $2,000 will have doubled to $4,000, while the seller will have lost his entire stake. Similarly, if the GNMA drops to 85 from 87, the buyer will have lost his $2,000, while the seller will have doubled his money.

Because of the high leverage, this is not investing and it is not speculating. It is *gambling*. The sale of GNMAs is a gamble with a lot going for it because inflation inevitably results in high interest rates, and higher interest rates will inevitably produce much lower prices for GNMAs.

The risk lies in the short-term fluctuation. It will do you no good to see GNMAs at a low of 80 one year from now if you are wiped out next week in a quick three-day move upwards. One can bet that there will always be short-term upward moves when the government finds it advisable politically to force down the interest rates artificially in an attempt to cure a bulge in unemployment or just prior to an election.

If you can afford a gamble and can sit out short-term fluctuations, I strongly recommend the sale of GNMAs at anywhere near their current levels. But if prices are way down before you read this book, then it is too late. After you have sold, put in an order to buy in if they move up two points—in other words, limit your loss to $2,000. If they start to move down, stay with it and pyramid. If you lose the first time round, try again when the price stabilizes. The idea is to limit your losses and let your profits rise.

Pyramiding is illustrated below:

DATE	BOUGHT	SOLD	COMMODITY	TRADE PRICE	SETTLEMENT PRICE	DEBIT	CREDIT
			BEGINNING LEDGER BALANCE				2,173.91
78-08-11		2	79JUN GINNIE MAE	906.875			
78-08-14		1	79JUN GINNIE MAE	905.312			
78-08-14		1	79JUN GINNIE MAE	907.187			
78-08-15		1	79JUN GINNIE MAE	904.062			
78-08-16		1	79JUN GINNIE MAE	899.375			

The first sales of GNMA were made at an average of $90\frac{6}{32}$. When the price reached $89\frac{31}{32}$ the paper profit was used to sell another GNMA. This increases the leverage many times and allows the opportunity to make huge sums from a small stake. If the June GNMAs were to move from 87 down to 76, this would increase the original $2,000 stake to $108,000 if completely pyramided.

I cannot stress strongly enough that GNMAs are gambling and very complex. *GNMAs are not for the novice.* But if you are going to gamble, I can think of few better chances for massive profits from limited capital.

Whatever Happened to Convertible Bonds?

Nothing illustrates recent changes in the investment climate better than convertible bonds. In 1966 I was describing convertible bonds as "the ideal investment," combining safety of capital together with a steady return and the possibility of capital gains. Today they are almost irrelevant to both investor and speculator. It is not that convertible bonds have changed, for they still have all the same characteristics that made them such a good vehicle in the sixties. No, it is the world around them that has changed—inflation has taken them right out of the picture.

A convertible bond is similar to any other corporation bond in that it is issued by a company in order to raise funds. It is a direct obligation of that company; it pays regular interest on the loan; and it must be repaid by a certain date, usually ten years later. Where the convertible varies from other bonds is that for a stated period during the life of that bond, the holder has the option to turn it in for common stock of the company at a price set at the time of issue and which is usually about 10% higher than the then market price. For example, Whisky Oil Company stock is trading at $18.50 per share and the company issues $10 million worth of 8% ten-year bonds, with each $1,000 bond being convertible into 50 shares of common stock at any time during the life of the bond. Obviously, there would be no point in immediate conversion because the stock would end up costing $20 per share and it can be bought on the open market at $18.50. So the buyer holds his bond and draws the 8% interest. But suppose one year later Whisky Oil makes a great strike and the stock moves up to $25 per share. Now the conversion feature becomes of great value, and since each bond can be changed into 50 shares, the $1,000 bond is now worth 50 times $25, or $1,250. In other words, if the stock goes down or stays the same, the holder just acts as though he has an ordinary bond, but if the stock goes up, he reaps large capital gains.

The reason convertibles are no longer an ideal investment is the same one that has ruined the attractiveness of ordinary bonds. Where the convertible holder originally had two fairly attractive options—make capital gains or sit still and draw interest—he now finds that one of the options is a disaster. Sitting still and drawing interest in inflationary times quickly destroys the investment. In other words, convertible bonds *per se* are no longer a good investment, but individual convertibles may still be attractive depending on the merits of the underwriting corporation.

In other words, if a solid oil company, gold mine or uranium company were to issue a convertible, it might be more attractive to buy the convertible rather than the common stock.

This is because convertibles have two major advantages over common stock. Firstly, the commissions are much smaller than on a comparable amount of stock. For example, if you buy $5,000 worth of convertibles, the commission will vary between $12.50 and $37.50 depending on the broker, but the commission on the same amount of stock will be somewhere between $70 and $100. Besides actually saving money, convertibles allow a speculator to trade profitably on very small moves.

Secondly, the amount of money required is much smaller than with stocks because only 25% margin (or less) is required instead of the 50% with stocks. This can result in very large and rapid profits. (See example on facing page.)

I was very pleased with my $190 profit on a $1,000 investment in just thirteen days, but looking back, I now realize I wasn't quite as smart as I had thought. One year later those same bonds that I had proudly sold at $91.50 went all the way up to $200! Oh well, no use crying over a profit.

Oil convertibles have been almost a sure source of profit. If you get a chance to get in on a new issue of oil convertibles, grab it, for it's amazing how rapidly profits can ensue. Here is one where I did fairly well:

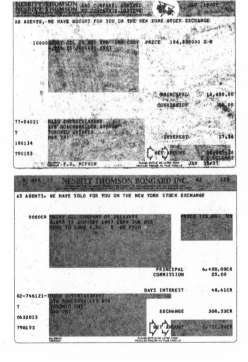

In summary, although convertibles are no longer the ideal investment, they still represent the chance to make a good profit *on certain occasions.* Buy them only if the underlying stock is one that you would buy if there was no convertible, but never, never buy one just because it is a convertible bond.

Options:
Strictly for Fools

Listed options are just that: options to buy or sell stock
that is listed on a stock exchange. A list of all the options
trading appears every day in *The Wall Street Journal* and
other financial papers.

An incredible number of options trade every day. On
the Chicago Board alone, 100,000 options trade daily and
there are over two million outstanding. Equally astonishing
figures are coming from the other exchanges.

There are three reasons for the great popularity of
options. Firstly, they are the newest game in town and have
received a great deal of favorable publicity, with frequent
stories of 50¢ options going to $15 in one week. Secondly,
they are extremely popular with one particular group of
people—the brokers, who handle the buying and the selling
—because they are making a small fortune out of them. And
finally, they are being traded in such volume mostly because
the public is stupid and has bought a phony bill of goods.

20 THE WALL STREET JOURNAL, Tuesday, Jan. 2, 1979

Chicago Board

Option	&	price	– Jan – Vol.	Last	– Apr – Vol.	Last	– Jul – Vol.	Last	N.Y. Close
Alcoa		.. 40	9	8¼	a	a	b	b	47¾
Alcoa		.. 45	30	3¼	12	5⅜	a	a	47¾
Alcoa		.. 50	233	7-16	39	2 5-16	a	a	47¾
Alcoa		.. 60	a	a	a	a	12	⅞	47¾
Am Exp		30	123	¾	13	1 9-16	a	a	29⅛
Am Tel		.60	4	1 3-16	96	2⅛	2	2⅞	60⅝
Am Tel		.65	2	1-16	72	½	41	1	60⅝
Atl R		.. 45	15	12⅜	a	a	b	b	56⅞
Atl R		...50	65	7⅛	40	8	33	9¼	56⅞
Atl R		...60	151	7-16	33	2⅜	14	3½	56⅞
Avon		45	12	7⅞	b	b	b	b	50¾
Avon	p	... 45	83	1-16	b	b	b	b	50¾
Avon		... 50	217	2¼	294	4	138	5¾	50¾
Avon	p	.. 50	636	1	168	2½	8	3	50¾
Avon		... 60	15	1-16	69	¾	28	1⅞	50¾
Avon	p	... 60	61	9	47	9½	a	a	50¾
BankAm		25	47	1	42	2	6	3	25¾
BankAm		30	1	1-16	6	7-16	2	⅞	25¾
Beth S		. 20	165	⅝	167	1½	73	2¼	19⅝
Beth S		. 25	30	1-16	75	⅜	13	13-16	19⅝
Bruns		...10	17	2¾	29	3¼	b	b	12⅝
Bruns		...15	456	1-16	162	11-16	b	b	12⅝
Bruns		...20	24	1-16	7	1-16	b	b	12⅝
Burl N		. 35	20	1	20	3½	a	a	35½
Burl N		. 40	44	⅛	34	1	38	1⅞	35½
Burl N		. 45	12	1-16	15	½	5	⅞	35½
Burrgh		..70	6	4⅞	a	a	a	a	73
Burrgh		80	44	7-16	15	2¾	1	5½	73
Citicp		...20	50	3	5	3¾	b	b	23½
Citicp		.. 25	174	3-16	133	1 1-16	156	1⅞	23½
Citicp		.. 30	28	1-16	22	3-16	20	11-16	23½
Delta		.. 40	43	2⅝	20	4½	6	5¾	41¾
Delta		. 45	97	¼	4	2⅜	a	a	41¾
Delta		. 50	8	1-16	18	13-16	a	a	41¾
Delta		.. 60	a	a	5	1-16	b	b	41¾
Dig Eq		40	43	13⅜	75	14¼	b	b	53⅝
Dig Eq		. 45	a	a	6	10⅜	a	a	53⅝
Dig Eq		50	106	3⅝	33	6¼	5	7⅞	53⅝
Disney		..35	a	a	a	a	2	7½	40¼
Disney		..40	11	1 7-16	a	a	a	a	40¼
Disney		. 45	385	⅛	2	1⅜	10	2 5-16	40¼
Dow Ch		20	7	5¾	17	5¼	b	b	25⅛
Dow Ch		25	220	⅞	169	2	b	b	25⅛
Dow Ch		30	176	1-16	290	7-16	b	b	25⅛
du Pnt		.110	4	16⅞	a	a	b	b	127
du Pnt		120	90	7¼	13	11¾	1	17¼	127
du Pnt		.130	94	1¾	3	6¾	a	a	127
du Pnt		.140	57	3-16	43	3	a	a	127
Eas Kd		45	12	15⅝	b	b	b	b	58¾
Eas Kd		.50	416	9½	192	11¾	57	12¾	58¾
Eas Kd	p	50	461	⅛	210	13-16	59	1½	58¾
Eas Kd		.60	2199	1 7-16	450	4½	210	6¼	58¾
Eas Kd	p	60	1399	2	314	4⅛	44	5	58¾
Eas Kd		.70	252	1-16	654	1⅛	117	2⅞	58¾
Eas Kd	p	70	74	10⅝	90	11½	95	10¾	58¾
Exxon		.. 40	a	a	7	9⅞	b	b	49⅛
Exxon		..45	25	4½	2	5½	10	6½	49⅛
Exxon		..50	395	⅝	258	1¾	9	2¾	49⅛
Exxon		.. 60	a	a	a	a	45	⅝	49⅛
F N M		. 15	33	1⅛	100	1⅞	a	a	16¼
F N M		. 20	a	a	266	⅛	3	½	16¼
Fluor		.. 30	34	3⅜	4	4¾	a	a	33½
Fluor		...35	28	9-16	4	2⅛	5	2⅝	33½
Fluor		.. 40	6	1-16	1	1-16	a	a	33½
Fluor		... 45	a	a	1	5-16	b	b	33½
Ford		40	13	2½	21	2⅞	b	b	42
Ford		45	164	1-16	110	1⅛	b	b	42
Ford		... 50	a	a	52	3-16	b	b	42
Gen El		. 45	57	2½	16	4	b	b	47⅛
Gen El		. 50	341	¼	46	1½	b	b	47⅛
Gen El		. 55	1	1-16	49	5-16	b	b	47⅛
Gen El		. 60	a	a	1	1-16	b	b	47⅛
G M		... 50	139	4⅝	70	6¼	b	b	54¼
G M	p	50	69	3-16	182	1½	b	b	54¼
G M		... 60	409	1-16	542	1	b	b	54¼
G M	p	60	396	5⅝	329	6½	b	b	54¼
G M		... 70	36	1-16	124	1-16	b	b	54¼
G M	p	... 70	a	a	5	15¼	b	b	54¼
Gt Wst		..20	1	6½	b	b	b	b	26⅝
Gt Wst		25	15	2¼	9	3⅝	12	4	26⅝
Gt Wst		. 30	5	1-16	16	1⅛	a	a	26⅝

Listed Options Quotations

Friday, December 29, 1978

Closing prices of all options. Sales unit usually is 100 shares. Security description includes exercise price. Stock close is New York or American exchange final price. p-Put option. o-Old shares.

Option	&	price	– Feb – Vol.	Last	– May – Vol.	Last	– Aug – Vol.	Last	N.Y. Close
Gen Fd		35	13	3-16	a	a	a	a	32⅛
Hewlet		..70	6	19¾	a	a	a	a	89⅞
Hewlet		. 80	78	10¾	1	14	1	15	89⅞
Hewlet		..90	193	4	50	7⅝	a	a	89⅞
Hewlet		.100	25	1⅜	90	3½	b	b	89⅞
H Inns		. 15	250	2¾	56	3¾	3	4⅛	16⅝
H Inns		. 20	532	11-16	86	1½	88	2	16⅝
H Inns		..25	299	⅛	103	½	b	b	16⅝
H Inns		..30	28	1-16	224	1-16	b	b	16⅝
H Inns		..35	12	1-16	a	a	b	b	16⅝
Honwll		..50	10	20⅝	a	a	a	a	69½
Honwll	p	50	173	1-16	39	5-16	40	1	69½
Honwll		. 60	338	10¾	69	13	1	15	69½
Honwll	p	60	645	11-16	153	2 1-16	20	3	69½
Honwll		. 70	473	3⅞	74	6¼	76	8¼	69½
Honwll	p	70	506	3¾	125	5⅝	25	6⅝	69½
Honwll		..80	347	⅝	236	2½	b	b	69½
Honwll	p	..80	19	10¼	a	a	b	b	69½
In Flv		..25	51	⅝	6	1¼	10	2 1-16	23⅝
In Flv		.. 30	5	1-16	a	a	b	b	23⅝
J Manv		20	4	3½	2	3⅞	18	4	22⅝
J Manv		25	89	½	15	1 1-16	15	1 11-16	22⅝
J Manv		.30	12	1-16	24	⅛	a	a	22⅝
MGIC		...20	7	¾	a	a	a	a	18⅜
MGIC		...25	4	1-16	41	⅞	b	b	18⅜
Mobil		.. 65	29	5½	a	a	a	a	69½
Mobil		...70	73	1⅜	17	3¼	2	4	69½
N Semi		15	2	6½	a	a	a	a	21¼
N Semi		.20	388	2 9-16	66	3¾	29	4¾	21¼
N Semi		.25	462	11-16	196	1 13-16	42	2½	21¼
N Semi		30	310	3-16	119	9-16	b	b	21¼
N Semi		35	36	1-16	210	5-16	b	b	21¼
Occi		 10	a	a	25	6¼	a	a	15¾
Occi		... 15	298	1 15-16	66	2 13-16	169	3¼	15¾
Occi		... 20	348	3-16	272	11-16	85	1 3-16	15¾
Occi		... 25	40	1-16	52	3-16	b	b	15¾
Occi		 30	5	1-16	b	b	b	b	15¾
Raythn		. 40	a	a	2	8⅜	a	a	46½
Raythn		. 45	7	3	51	5⅛	a	a	46½
Raythn		50	97	1⅛	105	3	5	4	46½
Raythn		. 60	15	1-16	6	13-16	b	b	46½
Rynlds		..60	65	9-16	25	1⅞	a	a	56⅝
Slumb		.. 70	2	26	b	b	b	b	94¾
Slumb		.. 80	47	16¼	a	a	a	a	94¾
Slumb		.. 90	271	8	5	11¼	a	a	94¾
Slumb		100	670	2¾	59	6¼	12	9½	94¾
Skylin		..10	93	1	13	1 9-16	39	2	10¼
Skylin		..15	67	1-16	22	5-16	25	⅝	10¼
Southn		..10	5	3⅜	a	a	a	a	13½
Southn		..15	8	1-16	21	⅛	40	⅜	13½
St Ind		.. 50	11	7¾	a	a	a	a	56⅝
St Ind		..60	14	⅜	1	1⅝	6	2	56⅝
Tx Glf		..20	23	⅝	29	1⅝	a	a	18½
Tx Glf		..25	a	a	5	¼	a	a	18½
U A L		..25	92	5	45	6⅜	51	7⅛	29⅛
U A L		..30	859	2⅛	302	3½	183	4⅞	29⅛
U A L		..35	1058	⅝	168	1¾	60	2⅝	29⅛
U A L		..40	420	⅛	84	11-16	b	b	29⅛
U A L		..45	31	1-16	115	⅜	b	b	29⅛
U Tech		. 35	26	5	a	a	a	a	38⅞
U Tech		40	48	1¾	25	3¼	a	a	38⅞
U Tech		45	53	5-16	3	1⅜	b	b	38⅞
U Tech		. 50	a	a	6	½	b	b	38⅞
U Tech		. 60	3	1-16	a	a	b	b	38⅞
J Walt		..25	a	a	10	3⅞	14	4⅝	26¾
J Walt		..30	27	7-16	1	1¼	a	a	26¾

Listed Options Quotations from The Wall Street Journal

Look at the first option on the list. It is an option to buy Aluminum Company of America at $40 and it is good until January. The stock closed that day at $47¾, and nine options traded with a final closing price of $8¼. This option is one that is "in the money" because the stock price is higher than the price at which the option can be exercised. Usually, option buyers seek out options that are not "in the money" because they are much cheaper and have far higher leverage. Look down the list two more lines and you will see options on the same company at $50, with the one expiring in January trading at only 44¢. Now just suppose you bought that option and Alcoa moved up to $60. Your 44¢ gamble is now worth $10. (Actually, they trade in hundreds and your $44 now becomes $1,000.) Wonderful, isn't it?

Who sells the options? A few are sold by gamblers who do not own any Alcoa and are willing to bet that the stock will not move above $50 in the few weeks the option has left to run. Most are sold by persons or institutions holding large stock portfolios who are trying to increase their income. It sounds as though the seller can't lose. Suppose you own 100 shares of Alcoa selling at $47¾ and you receive $44 for a twenty-day option on your stock. If the stock goes down, stays the same or moves up to $50, the option is not exercised and in twenty days you are back where you were before, still holding your stock but with an extra $44 in your pocket. On the other hand, if the stock moves above $50, the option will be exercised but you will receive $5,000 for your stock plus the $44 you received in advance, giving a net profit of $269 for twenty days. Sound good? Well, don't be in too much of a hurry to phone your broker.

A firm with which I worked did a study of some 150

option buyers and 38 option sellers. Among *all* option buyers, we found that they lost three-quarters of the time, and those persons buying options *regularly* ended up always as losers. But the most surprising results were concerning the option sellers. Each and every one of them showed a loss after two years of trading!

This really shouldn't be surprising if you stop to think about it. No new money is being created by an option. If the option buyer is betting that the price of the option will rise, then the option seller is betting the opposite. They can't both win. If the stock price drops, the buyer loses his entire stake; and if the stock soars and the option buyer makes a huge profit, this is money that the stockholder would have made if he had not sold his option. When it is all over, the profits of one group must exactly balance the losses of the other. But in actual fact, they don't, and this is the catch-22 of options. In every transaction the broker is taking his commission out of both sides, and that money has to come out of someone's pocket.

It is quite different from buying a stock, where if the company does well, the price of the stock rises, dividends are paid and everyone makes money. In options, no new money can be created. If you win, someone else must lose. It's just like a continuous poker game where the house takes 5% out of every pot. After a few hours some will have lost more than others, a few may be temporarily ahead, but if they continue to play in that situation, sooner or later the house ends up with all the money.

It's fairly obvious why option buyers do badly. Statistically, there is less than a 50% chance that Alcoa will reach $50.85, which is the break-even point for the option buyer ($50 plus 44¢ plus commissions), so that his occasional profits in a bull market just don't make up for the losses. The problem is that even if he guesses right and Alcoa moves up 10% in the twenty days, all he does is break even. If it just moves up 5%, he loses everything.

Note that it makes no difference if the option buyer picks a longer-running option. The Alcoa $50 option due next April trades at $2 5/16, and so the stock must move up much further in order to show a profit. If it goes in the wrong direction, the loss is much higher than with the cheaper option.

The reason option sellers end up as losers is not so clear, but basically they lose because markets are unpredictable. They don't just move up or down, but they gyrate in different directions, often with very short intervals. The result is that holders of stock portfolios who sell options get the worst of both worlds. In falling markets, as their stocks go down, they take massive losses cushioned only slightly by the option premium, but in rising markets, when they should be making huge profits, the options are exercised and they end up making only 5% or 10% profit on their investment. They limit their profits, but have unlimited losses. The option seller who attempts to trade his stock against the option can be murdered by a whipsawing market. In my more innocent days I sold an option against Molybdenum, and when the stock began to fall, sold out my position. Two weeks later the stock jumped back up above the option price and I was forced to buy it back to protect myself. Finally, one week before exercise date, the stock plunged below the option price! The final bill was $26,000.

It's a mugs' game! And don't listen to any broker who tells you different. He's making too much out of you to give you honest and disinterested advice.

There is one exception to my advice. If you have inside information on some company and don't mind breaking the law, you can make a great deal of money by buying an option before the public learns the news. It's done every week. A perfect example were the Husky Oil warrants, which surged from 50¢ to $13 in July 1978 when Petrocan made a takeover offer. Someone knew ahead of time and bought tens of thousands of warrants in advance of the offer, and I presume he is now basking in the tropical sun. Despite the frequency of this thievery, securities commissions are curiously reluctant to prosecute and I can't recall a single conviction since the Texas Gulf rip-off ten years ago. But if you are an insider and a crook, you don't need my advice.

Wine as an Investments

Many people have been forced to eat their words, but this is one area where the great danger is in drinking your investment. It is quite impossible to separate the pleasure of wine from its investment aspect, and perhaps this quality adds a special glow to the investment. After all, the lucky owner of a case of 1964 Petrus can joyfully drink one of his bottles and reflect that the eleven bottles that are left will still fetch at auction today double what he paid for the case last year. And if all other investments turn sour, wine will remain to give pleasure regardless of the owner's age or infirmity. If only other earthly pleasures persisted as long.

Of course, there is wine and there is wine, and most wines are not for investment. Also, wine investment is not for everyone, but if you have already protected yourself against inflation and would now like to be able to ensure pleasure and profit for your declining years, this is how to do it. I don't wish to hurt the sensibilities of American patriots who swear by the magnificent qualities of a California Sauterne or a New York red, but regardless of their qualities (and some California wines are magnificent), they are not for investment. You can't make a buck on them, simply because they rarely go up in price. The same applies to Italian wines, Chilean wines, Portuguese wines, almost all German wines and, oddly enough, most French wines.

What is left? About forty wines from the Bordeaux region, one or two from Burgundy, and perhaps the rarest wine of all, Trockenbeeren Auslese from Germany. We can dispose of the Trockenbeeren Auslese quickly enough because its initial high cost ($80 per bottle in a good vintage year) makes upward price movements difficult. If a 1976 Trockenbeeren Auslese sells for $80 today, and we expect to at least double our money on our investment every five years, we must look forward to someone being willing to pay $160 in 1984 for a bottle of an eight-year-old wine. Maybe it will happen, but I have my doubts.

The same applies to the great Burgundy—Romanée-Conti. This magnificent wine is produced in such small quantities that it is actually rationed to the wine stores. In order to get one case of Romanée-Conti, a wine merchant must purchase thirty cases of less remarkable wine. This results in very high prices to the customer, ranging from about $70 per bottle in the 1972 vintage to $250 for the 1976 vintage. It's pretty hard to move much higher to allow a profit when prices are so high to start. (A short time ago I saw a bottle of 1971 Romanée-Conti offered for sale in a Toronto restaurant for $650. There were no takers.) Anyone who buys Romanée-Conti or Trockenbeeren Auslese should not delude himself into calling it an investment— unless it be an investment in pleasure.

And this brings me to profiting in wine. To begin with,

one must buy wine that will not go bad as it gets older, that will go up in price and that can be resold at a profit. Many wines are pasteurized and will live forever, but because they are pasteurized they are in effect dead. They are second-rate and not worth a second glance—or taste. The non-pasteurized wines will continue to develop and grow in the bottle but will finally die of old age and turn to vinegar. The bottle life of most non-pasteurized wines is surprisingly short. Most whites last a few years at best, and Beaujolais and most red Bordeauxs don't live much longer. The finest Bordeaux, however, can last a hundred years or even longer, and the best of these develop so slowly that they are not even ready to drink for fifteen years and do not reach their peak for twenty-five years. The 1945 wines are an excellent example of these slow developers. They are finally at their peak today and will live for another fifty years (if given the chance).

Bordeaux wines from the Médoc were classified as to quality back in 1855, and the same classification is used today to grade these wines (with one change: Mouton-Rothschild was promoted a few years ago from second class to first). There are five classifications, and here are all the wines listed:

First Growth
Lafite-Rothschild   Mouton-Rothschild
Margaux   Haut-Brion
Latour

Second Growth
Rausan-Ségla   Lascombes
Rauzan-Gassies   Brane-Cantenac

Léoville-Las-Cases
Léoville-Poyferré
Léoville-Barton
Durfort-Vivens
Gruaud-Larose

Pichon-Longueville
Pichon-Lalande
Ducru-Beaucaillou
Cos-d'Estournel
Montrose

Third Growth

Kirwan, Cantenac
d'Issan, Cantenac
Lagrange, St.-Julien
Langoa-Barton, St.-Julien
Giscours, Labarde
Malescot-St.-Exupéry,
   Margaux
Cantenac-Brown, Cantenac

Boyd-Cantenac, Margaux
Palmer, Cantenac
La Lagune, Ludon
Desmirail, Margaux
Calon-Ségur, St. Estèphe
Ferrière, Margaux
Marquis d'Alesme-Becker,
   Margaux

Fourth Growth

St. Pierre, St.-Julien
Talbot, St.-Julien
Branaire-Ducru, St.-Julien
Duhart-Milon-
   Rothschild, Pauillac
Pouget, Cantenac

La Tour Carnet, St.-Laurent
Lafon-Rochet, St.-Estèphe
Beychevelle, St.-Julien
Prieuré-Lichine, Cantenac
Marquis-de-Terme,
   Margaux

Fifth Growth

Pontet-Canet
Batailley
Haut-Batailley
Grand-Puy-Lacoste
Grand-Puy-Ducasse
Lynch-Bages
Lynch-Moussas
Dauzac
Mouton-Baron-Philippe

du Tertre
Haut-Bages-Libéral
Pédesclaux
Belgrave
de Camensac
Cos-Labory
Clerc-Milon
Croizet-Bages
Cantemerle

There are many excellent wines in the second, third, fourth and fifth growths. (My favorites are Palmer and Talbot.) But from an investment point of view, it is best to stick to the first growth because there is always a ready market to sell these wines and they tend to increase faster in price than do their lesser neighbors. To these five great wines one should add two equally magnificent wines from the St. Émilion area, Cheval Blanc and Petrus, which have been and will continue to be excellent investments, and also one sweet wine, Château Yquem.

Collecting wine is not as easy as collecting Krugerrand. Although wine can be purchased and will be stored at nominal charge by the auction houses, one of the pleasures of wine ownership is keeping it in your own home, and for that a cool dark cellar is required where there is reasonable security and minimum temperature fluctuation. Also, remember that wine cannot be purchased on the basis of name alone, for the best vineyard will not produce great wine if the weather is bad and Bordeaux weather is always unpredictable. Thus you could have purchased a bottle of 1968 Lafite (a terrible year all over southern France) seven years ago for $5 a bottle and today you would get little more than your $5 back. (But if you had purchased a second-growth wine from a bad year, it could not be resold at any price.)

Here is a list of vintages as a general guide:

1961   Magnificent. Good for another hundred years.
1962   Average wines. Short life. Not good for investment.
1963   Awful.
1964   Good wines. Buy them if available cheap. Good for another twenty years.

1965   Awful.

1966   Good wines. Good investment. Good for our lifetime.

1967   Fair wines. Short life. Not for investment.

1968   Awful.

1969   Short life. Don't buy them.

1970   Magnificent. Up to now, second only to the 1961. If you can buy these at a fair price, do so.

1971   Good wines. Too short-lived for investment.

1972   Awful.

1973   Poor.

1974   Poor.

1975   The wines of the century. Buy them.

1976   Good wines. Too soon to judge longevity.

1977   Awful.

It is best to buy younger wines before the prices have soared, and probably the best buys for the investor today would be the 1975 and the 1970 vintages. The only problem with the 1975 vintages is that it is unlikely that many of my readers will ever drink these wines, for it is generally agreed that these great wines will not be ready for drinking before 1995. The middle-aged among us who buy such wines are really estate-planning rather than laying down a wine cellar. The 1970 vintages, on the other hand, will be drinkable in two or three years and will continue to improve for another ten or fifteen.

The place to buy these wines is not Bordeaux, since they are cheaper by a third to a half in New York City. Lafite 1970, for example, is sold at the châteaux for $45 per bottle but is freely available in New York at less than $30. The reason for this odd situation is the precipitous drop of the

U.S. dollar plus the imposition of large local French taxes. This is purely a temporary situation, and within the next year, as the effects of the dollar depreciation comes home to America, wine prices will move up sharply.

Currently, prices of the 1970 vintages are as follows in New York:

Lafite	$25 per bottle
Margaux	$24
Haut-Brion	$22
Latour	$23
Mouton	$24
Petrus	$40
Cheval Blanc	$29

Prices of the 1975 vintages are:

Lafite	$30 per bottle
Margaux	$24
Haut-Brion	$22
Latour	$30
Mouton	$26
Petrus	$45
Cheval Blanc	$30

You won't regret purchasing any of these.

As for buying old wines or selling your own collection, the best place is Christie's or Sotheby auction houses in London or Heublein in the United States. For $15 per year Christie's or Sotheby will send out a monthly catalogue listing all the wines for auction and giving their estimated prices, and after the sale they will tell you what the wines actually fetched. In addition, prior to each sale, they send out a newsletter giving valuable information about the wines available for purchase.

I have found Christie's to be a delight to deal with. Their service is excellent and commissions are very low (10% to 15%). They will either ship your wines or arrange storage.

NEWS FROM CHRISTIE'S WINE DEPARTMENT

SALE MEMORANDUM, SEASON 1978/9 No.1.

Finest & Rarest Wines & Collectors' Pieces - Thursday, September 21,1978

Foreword

Welcome, loyal old regulars and new subscribers, to the first major wine sale of the new season. In terms of range and quality, it is in the big league. A note about the contents below.

The original purpose of these sale memoranda - the first went out with our catalogue of October 11, 1966 - was to explain the difference between buying wine and works of art auction, to draw attention to the various services, and to give background information. As we invariably have a batch of new subscribers, and memories tend to be short, I propose to continue along the same lines.

Jet setting connoisseurs

This sale has a code reference 'Concorde II' to honour the small, elite and well-off ($4,746 for 7 days) group who are taking part in this year's 'Concorde' trip. Indeed, the theme 'Concorde to Champagne, Claret and Christie's', is reflected in the catalogue with a particularly good range of old classic vintages of champagne and of both the first growths at which the party will have dined: Lafite and Yquem. After the sale and a couple more banquets, they will wing it, supersonically, back to New York to liver salts and rest.

Contents of catalogue

I hope the general index to sections on the page preceding lot 1 will be a helpful lead-in. Further information follows:

Paris cellar, lots 24/41, 105/125, 153/169, 203/227 are all from a cellar in the heart of that city. The wines were laid down by the father of the present owner, a noted connoisseur. Incidentally, from the same cellar, came the first bottle of 1806 Lafite, taken by us to America for sale in 1976.

Unparalleled range of Lafite, lots 228/247 - a third bottle of the '06 (1806 that is), heads the magnificent collection of Lafite, which has come from another outstanding French cellar. The wines were inspected and packed in the original cellars by ourselves. Just to make one thing quite clear, they are not from Lafite, or from any other Rothschild cellar.

NB: overseas buyers can virtually ignore the dagger signs (necessary because the wine has been imported for sale) as the 8% value added tax is refundable on proof of exportation - we can advise and arrange.

One other excellent way to make money in wine is to buy for future delivery as soon as it is clear that the vintage is a great one. Thus, in August 1977, the Chicago Wine Company wrote their customers soliciting purchase of the 1975 first growths in these words:

> There has been a tremendous amount of interest and excitement about the 1975 Bordeaux vintage. The weather conditions during 1975 were very similar to what occurred in 1961—rain in the spring, a dry, hot summer and near-perfect weather during the harvesting. The sugar content of the grapes was high enough to ensure wines with an excellent balance of alcohol and acidity.
>
> While no one can guarantee that the wines from all of the châteaux will be as good as the fabulous 1961's, the reports are that a number of top-classified châteaux could equal or surpass the 1961's and possibly reach the level of the legendary 1929's and 1945's. As you probably already know, the 1961's are big, complex, long-lived wines that still, in many cases, have not reached their peak. Accordingly, the 1975's are wines to buy now for laying down for several years.

In the same mailing they included a table (see next page) to show how big profits were made in the great vintages of the past.

The wine company was right. The Petrus 1975 offered then at $20 has already doubled in price, and the other first growths have moved almost as much. It would have been nice to have bought 1975 futures, but it's too late for that. However, 1975 wines are still a good buy today.

What it all boils down to is that wine investment is a

Prices of Six Top Bordeaux Vintages
(Price per Case Converted to 1976 U.S. Dollars)

Vintage	Lafite Roth-schild	Latour	Mouton Roth-schild	Margaux
1929				
1st Offering to Importers	$18	$18	$18	$18
2nd Offering to Importers	$25	$22	$22	$22
Percentage Increase	38.9%	22.2%	22.2%	22.2%
1970 London Wholesale	$1,600	$850	$2,000	$500
1945				
1st Offering to Importers	$35	Data	$28	$45
2nd Offering to Importers	$50	not	$40	$50
Percentage Increase	42.9%	avail-	42.9%	11.1%
1970 London Wholesale	$850	able	$600	$600
1959				
1st Offering to Importers	$50	$30	$40	$35
2nd Offering to Importers	$75	$45	$50	$45
Percentage Increase	50.0%	50.0%	25.0%	28.6%
1970 London Wholesale	$800	$550	$625	$500
Average 1976 U.S. Retail (Approx.)	$1,380	$720	$1,200	$720
1961				
1st Offering to Importers	$80	$50	$60	$45
2nd Offering to Importers	$100	$90	$95	$75
Percentage Increase	25.0%	80.0%	58.3%	66.7%
1970 London Wholesale	$500	$425	$500	$360
Average 1976 U.S. Retail (Approx.)	$1,200	$1,020	$1,200	$1,020
1966				
1st Offering to Importers	$75	$60	$70	$50
2nd Offering to Importers	$100	$110	$120	$85
Percentage Increase	33.3%	83.3%	71.4%	70.0%
Average 1976 U.S. Retail (Approx.)	$350	$300	$350	$300
1970				
1st Offering to Importers	$110	$75	$115	$80
2nd Offering to Importers	$150	$145	$160	$135
Percentage Increase	36.4%	93.3%	39.1%	68.8%
Average 1976 U.S. Retail (Approx.)	$300	$290	$290	$265

luxury because time and patience are needed for prices to rise and will power is essential to keep from drinking the investment. But for a small portion of your funds, this brings a charm that can be found nowhere else in life—and occasionally a most unexpected profit. Just last month I discovered that the Liquor Control Board in my area, which normally overcharges everybody, had put on sale 150 cases of Château Palmer 1970 at $12.70 a bottle, while the same wine was selling simultaneously in London at $30 per bottle. One entrepreneur builder friend purchased twenty cases of the Palmer, which he is shipping to London for auction. I bought nine cases and am torn between cupidity and desire for the wine. Such an unusual windfall couldn't happen in any other investment field.

How much profit can one reasonably expect to make by investing in wine? At the worst, your investment should keep up with inflation. With a little luck, another boom will develop in French wines and today's $20 bottle of wine could easily go to $100. After all, a Latour in a good year should be worth as much as a Romanée-Conti or a Trockenbeeren Auslese. One thing for sure, because of inflation you won't lose money.

Higher wine prices in France are not an isolated event: inflation is affecting many things other than wine, and Europe is way ahead of us. In August 1978 I priced a traveling clock in the Cartier shop in Bordeaux at $285, and one week later saw the same clock in Cartier's New York store for $195. Cartier has not gone crazy. This variance in price is due to the extreme fall in the dollar, which shows no sign of stopping.

These discrepancies are temporary and they are not going to be solved by European prices falling. Instead, we are already seeing a flood of German and Swiss tourists taking advantage of our low prices, and this will end the same way it did in Britain when the pound fell. Prices in the United States will rise to meet foreign levels. If there is something you will have to buy soon, don't wait. It will cost you more next spring.

And this brings me to the most pleasant investment of all—beautiful things.

Art and Antiques: Investment to Love

The sketch on the following page was made in Peking in 1780. I bought it in 1976 for $10. The shawl cost me $400 in Spain the year before that. It was made in the Philippines immediately after World War I. The golden cup was made in Russia in 1880 for the Romanoffs. In 1979 it was purchased in Toronto for $2,000. The box was made in 1800 for some wealthy Polish aristocrat. It was bought in New York recently for $7,000.

All of these objects represent the opportunity to profit in coin and pleasure at the same time. The sketch has multiplied in value ten times in just three years; the value of the shawl has doubled in the same period. The owner of the cup was offered $2,800 only three days after his purchase. And the box was just resold for $9,000. Even more

important, ownership of such beautiful objects brings
constant pleasure and excitement.

The important word in the last paragraph is "beautiful,"
for with the great variety of art and antiques available for
investment today, the objects that move up consistently in
price are those that are considered beautiful. It is true that
ideas of beauty vary drastically from person to person, but
some things are universally accepted as beautiful—well,
almost universally. Three years ago I brought out a book
on investing in art[1] and I was amazed at how deep were
the passions that I stirred. Some people don't like the
thought of anyone buying art in order to profit, for they
feel it's somehow indecent. This attitude was summed up
by a scathing condemnation of my book in the August 1977
issue of an artsy magazine called *Saturday Night*:

> Art collecting, as Shulman practises it, is itself a parody
> of capitalism. It is capitalism stripped of all social justifica-
> tions. It does nothing but turn a profit. It provides no
> jobs, builds no cities, pays few taxes—Shulman rejoices
> in the fact that governments haven't yet figured out how
> to tax art. It doesn't lead to the creation of distinguished
> collections which can later be enjoyed by whole com-
> munities—in this kind of art investing, collections are
> constantly being broken up, the individual pieces being
> passed on from collector to dealer to collector. It of course
> supports no acts of creation; it specifically avoids just
> that kind of thing, on the grounds of high risk, and
> thereby surrenders the act of patronage, the main justi-
> fication for art collecting during the last few centuries.
> It is capitalism-for-capitalism's sake, a queer kind of

[1] *Anyone Can Make Big Money Buying Art* (New York: Macmillan;
Toronto: Fitzhenry & Whiteside, 1977).

inversion of the art-for-art-sake's doctrine that Shulman would probably find abhorrent. *Anyone Can Make Big Money Buying Art*, if it happens to be read by somebody a century from now, will be identified quickly as a mean-minded Marxist's parody of the acquisitive instinct, misleadingly and mischievously issued under the name of a famous millionaire socialist of the day.

And far from finding my art objects beautiful, the writer of the column, one Robert Fulford, lumped them all together as "kitsch."

Well, perhaps I am a philistine by art-world standards, but I don't think that there is some mortal sin in investing in a painting as compared to a gold bar or in an ancient glass cup instead of a stock certificate. The critics don't like it, but an errant capitalist can get just as much pleasure from a beautiful old Syrian cup as a collector of modern art may get from his dabs of incomprehensible (to me) paint. Anyway, enough of the critics. The important thing is that during periods of rising inflation, one of the safest ways to protect capital is to invest in art. Everything else may go to pot, but good art keeps its value.

But what art should one buy? Paintings or sculpture, old furniture or stained glass, armor or silver, Chinese art or Russian art, watches or glass—there is enough variety for every taste. And that answers the question: buy what you like, what turns you on. With so much available, there's no point in collecting things you don't enjoy. But if you want to be sure to profit, you must follow certain guidelines, just as in any other type of investment.

First of all, old is better. Don't buy *any* modern art for investment. It's not that our contemporaries won't produce items of lasting value, just as every society that has preceded us has done. It's that we're too close to the vast mass of today's art to tell what will last and what will not. It was the same with every preceding generation. Just look back to paintings done a hundred years ago; ninety-nine percent of them are practically unsalable today, even though many of them sold for large sums when first produced. Also, today's more prominent living artists are heavily promoted by their supporting galleries, and the prices are carefully controlled and pushed upwards to levels that appear totally unreasonable in relation to the prices for the works of the great artists of yesteryears.

Hundertwasser is an example of this trend. This very popular young artist now issues signed engravings, with perhaps three hundred copies, which his New York gallery sells at around $2,000. Compare that to Picasso's *Vollard Suite*, of which there were three hundred copies made forty-five years ago and which are available for a third less than a Hundertwasser. Or go back a long way to Rembrandt's engravings, which sell for as little as $1,000. Such inequities can't last indefinitely, so it's extremely unlikely that anyone buying Hundertwasser today will make a profit. This doesn't mean modern art should never be purchased; but don't do it for investment purposes. If something turns you on and you will get sufficient pleasure from it, that is a different matter entirely. But don't kid yourself into thinking it's an investment.

Among old things, small is far better than large. Tiny objects appreciate in value anywhere from three to ten times as quickly as unwieldy things. So buy a watch instead of a clock, old jewelry instead of old furniture, snuff boxes instead of old chests. The reason is a basic one. Art for investment is collected by a wide variety of wealthy and not so wealthy individuals, many of whom live in politically unstable areas like the Middle East, and if these collectors have to run, they want to be able to take their wealth with them. The people of Europe have learned from repeated wars that many persons who could stuff their valuables into a suitcase saved that wealth (and sometimes their own lives as a result), while persons of comparable wealth that was invested in land, furniture and "grand" possessions lost everything. The Junkers of East Prussia are the perfect example. Those who put their money into baronial possessions were stripped in 1945, while those who had invested in small art objects were able to escape with them, and with financial resources, were able to begin again in the West.

It is unlikely anyone will ever have to flee from Chicago or any other U.S. city, but that doesn't matter. Since valuable art objects are internationally auctioned, the higher bids coming from overseas push up the prices in North America as well. It isn't just Europeans and Arabs who want smaller valuables. The people of Canada and Mexico have seen their currency collapse in recent years, and from both countries there has been a flight of wealth plus the accumulation of small precious objects. This may well end with currency controls in both countries and a ban on the export of assets. But how can any government keep track of a two- or three-inch privately owned object, no matter how valuable it may be. Precious small objects are becoming the ultimate refuge for nervous wealth all over the world, and as a result, their value goes up steadily as the dollar continues its decline.

Old, small and beautiful. What else should we look for? Innate value certainly helps. Objects containing gold or precious stones are more likely to retain their value in bad times and go up in good times than something like a painting whose value is just in its beauty. Chinese export silver made of pure silver and beautifully enameled, for example, was always salable for its silver value in China and Hong Kong, even during the 1948 debacle when exquisite paintings and porcelain vases were simply abandoned. I purchased the set of silver spoons shown below from the Chinese government for their weight in silver ($70) just three years ago when that country was selling off so much of its art. Today it would bring at least four times that figure.

Beware of fakes. This is the great pitfall in art investing and is amazingly common. No one need ever get stuck with a fake, for local museums are happy to authenticate (but not evaluate) any object. And of course, you should not be buying for investment in any antique store, even the best. Their markup is too high to leave room for you to profit and prices must go up by at least 50% before you are back to even. The two big advantages in buying from the big international auctioneers are that prices are basically at the wholesale level. There is also no danger of buying a fake because the auctioneers give a guarantee of authenticity.

You have five years to claim your money if it turns out the piece is not real.

The New York addresses of the three big international auction houses that sell to the public are:

Phillips, 867 Madison Ave., New York 10021.

Sotheby Parke Bernet, 980 Madison Ave., New York 10021.

Christie, Manson & Woods, 502 Park Ave., New York 10022.

All of these companies will be happy to put readers on their mailing lists of forthcoming sales at no charge. Individual catalogues may be purchased, or for a few dollars a subscription may be ordered for all the sales in the desired field.

The one reason to justify buying in antique shops is to fill out a particular hole in a collection, or because an object is so beautiful that temporary overpayment is worthwhile. Over the years I have purchased several such magnificent and unique pieces from the likes of A La Vieille Russie or Skala's in New York, Wartski in London and Au Vieux Cadran in Paris, and have ended up with my acquisition being worth far more than I paid, because during times of inflation the best pieces go up the fastest.

And that is very important. Regardless of the price range you are working in, always buy the best piece available that you can afford. Second-rate artworks are hard to get rid of and slow to appreciate in value, but there is always a ready market for the best.

How much return should one expect from an investment in art? Profits can be fantastically large here, higher than in any other field. But patience is necessary, and it is rare to turn something over in a few days. For the investor who is prepared to wait for three to five years, amazing profits are possible. The largest profit I ever made in the stock market was in a little company called Canada Foils, when my $350 investment turned into $16,500. That great gain looks small beside the watch I bought for $250 and sold for $65,000! That was, of course, highly unusual, but an astute art investor should do at least as well as the investor in land or gold. He has one extra advantage that can be found nowhere else: he is guaranteed a profit.

The way to do this is to work closely with your local museum. Buy something that your museum wants to own (every museum curator is happy to advise on buying such objects), retain and enjoy your purchase for two or three years while inflation pushes up its price, and then donate it to the museum and take a tax deduction. You will be allowed a valuation dependent on the current fair retail market value of the art object. If you have bought reasonably at auction, you can make just as big a profit this way as by resale—and with no risk!

In summary, art investment offers the excellent possibility of huge profits associated with many dividends in the form of pleasure. Of course, there is always the chance of falling in love with your purchase, and then selling becomes too painful. The most beautiful thing I own is a lovely eighteenth-century pendant made of pearls and filigree gold with a seven-day watch on its back. Made originally for a mistress of Louis XVI and sold for the equivalent of $180 dollars (equivalent to many tens of thousands of today's dollars), it disappeared during the revolution and reappeared after World War II. In 1945 it was brought to a Parisian dealer, Madame Aug Seiler, by a French general's widow, and she purchased it for 800 francs (about $200). Ten years later a famous New York watch-shop owner

named Mr. Barney saw the piece at Madame Seiler's and bought it for $350. In 1964 I bought it from him for $1,000. Two years ago I turned down a $100,000 offer for the pendant.

Where else can an investor find such romance and excitement?

Oil and Taxes: For Millionaires Only

———◆•◆———

It is obvious that if one is to move ahead financially, tax payments should be kept to the legally possible minimum. I have touched on cutting taxes and making a profit by giving away art objects to the local museum. There are many other legal gimmicks available to reduce income taxes, but these are outside the province of this book. There is one method, however, that is intimately tied in with inflation and "wealth in the ground" that should be given consideration here—investing in oil drilling.

Governments recognize the necessity of increasing our oil and gas reserves and for that purpose encourage exploration by giving generous tax write-offs to persons who invest money in this field. As a result, oil drilling has become a very, very attractive speculation today. To make clear how very attractive it is, let us suppose an investor puts $5,000 into shares of the XYZ oil company listed on the New York Exchange and the company goes broke. The end result is simply that the investor has lost his $5,000 and there is no compensation available to him, although he may deduct that $5,000 from any capital gain he has made when computing his capital-gain tax. Let us suppose, instead, that that same investor takes his $5,000 and invests it in a private oil-drilling fund which also goes broke. The end result here is quite different. Under current laws the entire $5,000 can be deducted from the investor's income before calculating his tax, so the government actually pays over half of the loss!

This chapter is headed "For Millionaires Only" because private drilling funds don't want to bother with small investors. Most of them will take only minimum investments of $50,000 or $100,000, although there are a few that will take as little as $15,000.

In the fall of 1978 I was approached by the president of the Alberta Stock Exchange, Bob Peters, who urged me to put $100,000 in a new private drilling fund being underwritten by his company. The fund is called Sceptre Resources Partnership. It is run by a general partner in the form of a well-established public company called Sceptre Resources, which is active in the oil drilling and development business in western Canada. Its stock is listed on the Toronto Stock Exchange. The setup is quite typical of such funds. Twenty-five or more limited partnerships were being sold at $100,000 each. Sceptre Resources uses the money, plus their own funds, in the ratio of 70% from the limited partners and 30% from Sceptre Resources, to buy land and drill wells. All revenue is shared equally by Sceptre Resources and the limited partners. If Sceptre loses, the loss is deductible from the investors' income tax.

It is very intriguing, but obviously no one goes into an investment expecting to lose and take a tax deduction, so the key is, really: What are the chances of profit? It all boils down to with whom you are investing. I examined the record of Bob Peters' seven previous drilling funds and was amazed to discover that so far all of these have been profitable, so that none of his investors has had to depend on the tax deduction. His past funds were as follows:

(1) Kildonan 1976 Fund. Now earning $200,000 per year for every $100,000 invested. $600,000 was originally invested and another $1,900,000 was borrowed. Over the next twelve years it is forecast that this will grow to $11,000,000.

(2) Kildonan 1977 Fund. The $2 million put in this fund are still being spent. But already they have successfully drilled one oil well and three gas wells. The success so far indicates that the investors will have all their own money back by 1983.

(3) Concept Drilling Partnership. This fund was started only one year ago, but already they have proven up and capped a gas field worth at least double the original investment.

(4) Westlock Joint Venture. This fund was organized in late 1976 to take advantage of Alberta's income tax incentive cash rebates. Individuals in the 58% personal-income tax bracket ended up having no after-tax investment in this program. To date, sales from the fund have totaled $625,000. Earned depletion of $200,000 is available from resource income to a maximum of 25%, resulting in a taxable income of $475,000. Thus, after

tax, investors ended up earning $249,500. Subsequent sales will increase the percentage return from this wonderful investment where the invested capital is zero.

(5) Willesden Green Joint Venture. This program is identical in structure to the Westlock program, but has not been as financially rewarding. The pre-tax investment of $225,000 again worked out to zero after tax investment. However, revenues on this smaller program have totaled only $90,000 to date.

(6) CRA Ocelot Fund. The CRA Ocelot Fund has been sold to the operator for a gross 20% pre-tax return and estimated (depending upon individual income tax rate) 35% after tax return.

(7) CRA Exploration 78 Program. Because this fund is only a few months old, there are no results as yet.

Obviously, not every drilling fund is going to have Bob Peters' success—nor is he likely to continue to bat a thousand. I asked Peters what rules he lays down for his funds, and he listed six:

(1) The programs must have the potential for a minimum annual 20% after tax return.

(2) The operator must share the monetary risk associated with the expected return.

(3) The underwriters must invest their pre-tax dollars alongside and on the same basis as the investors.

(4) All funding should be done via private placements to avoid the time loss and cost of regulatory scrutiny. (I don't agree with this. Regulation is needed to protect against crooks.)

(5) The sharing of the reward after the investor has recovered his capital cost is weighted in the investor's favor, not that of the operator and/or the promoter.

(6) The operator-manager of the program represents the best talent available.

My rules to success in this exciting investment field are simple:

(1) It helps to be in a high tax bracket.

(2) You must have a large amount of cash available that can be tied up for several years. You can't sell out the way you could if you were in stocks.

(3) All these funds have a general partner who manages the pot. The key to whether you invest should be the track record of the general partner.

(4) Look at the prospectus and see if the underwriter has invested his own money. If the deal is a fair one, he should be willing to risk his own funds.

Anyone following these rules in a drilling fund is likely to get very rich. At the worst, the U.S. government will be happy to share the losses.

Postage Stamps and Coins: For the Collector

———•••———

Stamps

Perhaps surprisingly, one of the best inflation hedges has proven to be old stamps. The total value of every unused U.S. postage stamp between 1882 to 1909 rose from $4,444 in 1954 to $39,389 in 1977. This is a rise of 786%, which far outperformed the stock market (and even gold) during that period. The boom in stamps shows no sign of slowing down, for the 1979 Scott Catalogue shows an average 20% rise in the price of classic U.S. stamps since 1978. Airmail stamps from before the war have done even better. Here are some examples from Scott Catalogues:

UNITED STATES

Cat. No.	Issue	Date	1979 Percentage Increase Over 1978
C7-C9	Map	1926/27	76.60
C10	Lindbergh	1927	57.89
C11	Beacon	1928	30.77
C12	Winged Globe	1930	37.14
C13-C15	Graf Zeppelin	1930	32.84
C16,C17,C19	Winged Globe, rotary press	1931/34	28.81
C18	Zeppelin	1933	37.50
C20-C22	Clipper	1935/37	63.51
C20	Clipper	1935	37.50
C21	Clipper	1937	78.57
C22	Clipper	1937	57.89
C24	Wings	1939	17.65

It is not just U.S. stamps that have proven so profitable. Canadian issues have done even better:

CANADA

Cat. No.	Issue	Date	1979 Percentage Increase Over 1978
158	Bluenose	1928/29	29.63
158a	Bluenose Imperforate	1928/29	114.29
159	Parliament	1928/29	25.00
159a	Parliament Imperforate	1928/29	87.50
160-161	Scroll Coils	1929	25.02
162-172	Arch	1930/31	37.53
162-175	Arch & Pictorial	1930/31	45.70
162-177	Arch & Pictorial	1930/31	57.63
174a-177a	Pictorial Imperforate	1930/31	60.00
178-183	Arch Coils	1930/31	32.59
184	Admiral Perforated 12X8	1931	20.00
190	Cartier	1931	50.06
190a	Cartier Imperforate	1931	25.00

Cat. No.	Issue	Date	1979 Percentage Increase Over 1978
191, 191a	George V Arch Surcharge	1932	49.81
192–194	Conference	1932	55.44
195–201	Medallion	1932	74.58
195c–200a	Medallion Imperforate	1932	17.65
195c–201a	Medallion Imperforate	1932	31.58
201a	Medallion Imperforate	1932	60.00
202	UPU	1933	50.00
203	Grain Exhibition	1933	50.00
204	Royal William	1933	40.00

The reason for this tremendous boom is purely and simply inflation. Investors are seeking out things that will hold their value as the dollar sinks. There are far more people buying postage stamps than any other collectible simply because tens of thousands of adults learned their expertise from their childhood hobby. Also, it is far easier to invest in stamps than, for example, in old snuffboxes, since all stamps are catalogued but every snuffbox has a different value.

There are a few basic rules:

(1) Specialize. It is hard enough to learn about the stamps of one country, so don't attempt to cover the world. It is always best to collect the stamps of your own nation.

(2) Buy only old stamps, the older the better. There is no profit to be made in collecting modern commemoratives that are turned out by the million.

(3) Buy only perfect copies. Damaged stamps will sell for a tiny fraction of the catalogue price and are extremely slow to rise in price.

(4) Mint stamps go up in price faster than used ones. And if you are buying mint copies, buy ones that have not been hinged.

(5) Avoid the stamps of defunct countries; they tend to have too few collectors to produce a wide market.

(6) Do patronize the auction houses. Their prices tend to be lower than dealers' prices.

Many persons who do not have the confidence or the knowledge to buy stamps for themselves are now investing in them through stamp investment firms such as Universal Stamp Corporation. These companies have made a great deal of money in the last five years by selling packages in amounts ranging from $500 to $250,000 to investors who leave the choice of the stamps up to the investment company. All of the companies offer to repurchase their stamps at any time at the current market price. Because of the inflation boom, all of their clients have made money so far. Universal boasts that:

Clients who held them for more than twenty-four months always made a substantial gain. The average gain for clients who resold their stamp shipments back to us after twenty-four to thirty-six months was 63%, with the lowest gain being 35.28% and the highest gain 90.91%. Clients who held them for more than three years have in no case made less than a 70% gain. The average gain of clients in cases of such repurchases was 88%. The highest gain was 106%.

An investor will do better investing on his own provided he has the required knowledge about these little bits of paper. Obviously, all the investment companies in this business are there to make money for themselves. If, however, an investor has no expertise, an investment company offers a reasonable alternative.

Stamps vs. Purchasing Power of the Dollar[1]

From January 1969 to December 1977, the purchasing power of the dollar declined by more than 40%. Prices of selected fine stamps showed an average annual increase in value of over 20%, thus an increase of over 200% during this period.

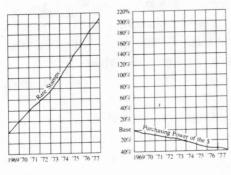

Reprinted with permission from Amberley Investment.

Coins

In recent years, coin collecting has boomed, but just as in the stamp field, one must be discriminating. I have already discussed collecting coins for their gold content, but except for gold coins, it is plain foolish to collect any modern coinage. It just isn't possible for any scarcity value to develop and the metal value of today's coins is only a fraction of their face value. This leaves for consideration old coins from the United States or ancient coins. While it is true that in recent years prices in this area have gone up by about

---

[1] Reprinted by permission of Universal Stamp Corporation.

15% annually, it is not easy to value or to sell these coins at anywhere near retail prices. Price depends upon both scarcity and condition. But the biggest hazard in this field is that it is now plagued by forgeries, some of which are so good, it is almost impossible to distinguish them from the real thing. *Unless you are a real expert, I would warn investors away from old coins.*

There is one relatively safe way the amateur can invest in old coins. Bowers & Ruddy Galleries, a subsidiary of General Mills, has set up a collector's investment program. The investor deposits $100 per month or more and receives in return diversified collections of U.S. coins of various dates, sizes and series. There is no guarantee as to how well they will do in the future, but their past record is impressive, showing an average gain of 20% per year since 1974.

Another way for the amateur to enter this field is through a limited partnership in a rare-coin fund. Guardian Corporation of Southington, Connecticut, in September 1979 underwrote such a fund, which is quite similar to a mutual fund but all the investments are in rare U.S. coins. This fund is managed by Boston's New England Rare Coin Management, Inc.

This is certainly not my first choice as an inflation hedge, but if collecting coins turns you on, this is an easy way to begin.

Memorabilia and Other Bad News for Investors

Inflation is invariably accompanied by fiscal madnesses in investments—as well as in paper money—and memorabilia is a perfect example. Memorabilia is nostalgia, things that have no real value but remind people of their youth. Articles of memorabilia invariably become sought after when paper money loses its value. Thus, old comic books can sell for thousands of dollars, a Mickey Mouse watch can bring $250 and an Elvis Presley doll recently sold for $1,000. The same phenomenon took place during the great German inflation, with General Ludendorf dolls selling for thousands of marks, but just fifteen years later the price of Germany's memorabilia from the Kaiser's time totally collapsed, never to recover. The reason is simple enough. Memorabilia holds its value only so long as collectors from that era retain their nostalgia. As that generation of collectors begins to die off, so does the demand for the junk of their youth.

I cannot advise my readers strongly enough—*memorabilia is a foolish place to put money.* Even depreciating cash is a better speculation than old baseball cards, toys, beer cans or Coca-Cola signs.

Limited Editions

Limited editions are just as bad, and it seems as though every current magazine carries an ad for a new limited edition of something. The sad fact is that although a lot of money has been made from limited editions, it has almost all gone into the pockets of the manufacturers of this new craze. The Franklin Mint began the whole thing, and they now have a lot of imitators who produce objects designed to appeal to the desire for real things during an inflation. The problem with these real things is that they are sold far above their actual value, and because they are being continually poured into the market, no true scarcity can develop. A recent survey showed that most purchases from these mints cannot be resold at cost let alone show a profit.

The appeal made to investors in ads for limited editions is quite clever. Here is a pitch from an issue of *Money Magazine*:

The special attraction of collector's plates is that they are original, limited-edition works of art as well as a measurable investment with a well-established secondary market. The most prized editions have outperformed even the most glamorous securities.

Plate collecting possesses many unique advantages not found in other forms of art collecting and investments. Unlike stamps and coins, collector's plates are original works of art issued in limited edition. They are meant to be displayed and appreciated, while stamps and coins are hidden away in albums. Most importantly, no stamp or coin is usually issued as a limited edition, while every collector's plate is.

A comparison with antiques is misleading. Even the oldest collector's plates aren't antiques by the generally accepted definition. And the fast-moving market in plates hardly compares with the slow, involved trading of antiques.

These appeals are amazingly successful. According to the same ad, there were 2.2 million collectors of these plates in the United States as of the end of 1977 and they estimate that figure will double this year.

And all of this proves that Barnum was right!

Photographs

Collecting old photos is being aggressively promoted by a few galleries, but if ever there was a bubble about to burst, this is it. Any photograph can be reproduced by a clever technician, with or without a negative, in unlimited amounts. This area is not for intelligent investors.

Autographs

This is an interesting hobby but hardly the place to put serious money. The market is too thin and dealers mark-ups are far too high.

Dolls

Same situation. Okay as a hobby; lousy as an investment.

Books

A very important and booming field, but too much specialized knowledge is required. The amateur should leave this one to professionals.

Rugs

Too late. Prices have already gone to dizzy and, in my opinion, unrealistic levels.

Pension Plans

It amazes me how many otherwise sensible people are sinking today's relatively good dollars into pension plans that will pay off in twenty or thirty years. The rationale is supposed to be that no taxes are paid on contributions until they are withdrawn from the plan in the future and in the meantime the moneys pile up interest. In normal times a Keogh pension plan would make sense, but in a bad inflation most pension plans are no good for the same reason bonds are no good. They will pay off in worthless paper money.

The only pension plans that make any sense are those that are self-managed and in which equity is placed in the form of gold, land or other real things. Alas, these sensible pension plans make up less than a fraction of the 1% of all the pensions extant.

Let me repeat, *Keoghs only make sense if the moneys deposited are used to buy inflation-proof investments.* Any of those described in this book are suitable, such as stamps, coins or antiques. The best is probably gold, because it has the smallest initial markup from its resale value.

Three Plans
to Follow

———•◆•———

Even for those who understand inflation, the route to
financial success is not obvious, because there are so many
possible roads to follow. This book has talked about gold
and antiques, stamps and coins, real estate and GNMAs—
but where and how should one start and what proportion
of money should go into each type of investment? That key
question will be answered differently depending on the
investor's age, resources and responsibilities. I have, therefore, laid out three different options for my readers. For
most people there is no salvation from the forthcoming
financial disaster simply because they have nothing with
which to work. Every time I appear on an open-line show
the first telephone question I receive is invariably "What
should someone do who has nothing to invest?" I can only
reply, "With nothing, you can do nothing except pray for
a miracle." The terrible truth is that the vast majority of
people in the United States fall into this category. However, it is unlikely that many of them will read this book.

Who are my readers? Coneducor, a company for which I write and that has sold tens of thousands of courses in investing in the United States, did a survey and determined that a typical subscriber was male, age forty-two, married, with two children. His annual income ranges from $15,000 to $30,000 and his net worth is $125,000 to $150,000, consisting mainly of an equity in a personal residence, plus $10,000 to $15,000 in a locked-in pension plan, plus about $10,000 to $20,000 in other investments. His annual savings consists of $3,000 to $4,000 in cash, plus a gradual increase in equity in his home. His occupation is middle management in a large corporation, or he is a professional, such as a doctor, dentist or engineer (but he is not an accountant), or the owner of a small independent business. His I.Q. tends to be higher than the average and he tends to be relatively sophisticated about finance.

This investor has the most to lose from inflation, for it is this category that has suffered the worst from previous inflations, and yet this is the investor who has the resources to protect himself by using his equity more wisely. For him, I suggest plan one.

Plan One

You own a home purchased ten years ago for $75,000 which is now worth $160,000 and on which there is still a $35,000 mortgage. You have $12,000 in a pension plan which you can't touch and you own $15,000 in government bonds and blue-chip stocks. In addition, you have about $10,000 in equity in whole life insurance and you have $2,000 or $3,000 tied up in a hobby—stamps or coins, antiques, jewelry or Oriental rugs, or dolls. In whatever field it is, presumably it is one in which you have developed some expertise. This is what you should do:

(1) Purchase enough term insurance to cover your family's needs for the next five years and then cash in your whole life insurance. Don't cash in the insurance first, just in case you are no longer insurable.

(2) If your pension plan is cashable, cash it in even if this requires paying an immediate tax.

(3) Sell your government bonds and blue-chip stocks.

(4) Renegotiate your mortgage, increasing it to the *maximum* on which you can afford to meet the payments from your *current* income.

After the previous maneuvers have been completed, you should have approximately $100,000 in cash. I would invest this as follows:

(1) $5,000 in Krugerrand, which should be kept in a safety deposit vault.

(2) $15,000 divided between "wealth in the ground" stocks such as Dome Mines, Campbell Red Lake, Homestake, Denison, International Nickel, Pacific Pete, Hudsons Bay Oil & Gas or Imperial Oil, with most of it going into the first three.

(3) $55,000 into gold bullion.

(4) $20,000 into your hobby, be it stamps, coins or whatever, provided:

(a) Your hobby is not a fad—such as photography or memorabilia.

(b) You know that you have the knowledge and experience.

(c) There is an international market for your purchases.

(d) You buy only the best pieces.

(5) The last $5,000 should be used in an attempt to grab the brass ring. The average amateur tries to do this by buying lottery tickets. You will have much better odds for your money if you put this $5,000 into the currency or commodity market, buying gold, Swiss francs or German marks. You may lose your $5,000, but you just might walk away with a million.

Plan Two

My second largest category of readers is the widow class. She is fifty to sixty years old and has been left an estate of $175,000 by her husband, most of which was in the form of insurance plus an equity in a house, and she has had little or no financial experience. By the time she seeks my advice, she has sold the home and has invested the entire sum in government bonds. I am often consulted by such ladies, but they rarely, if ever, follow my advice because "I need the money invested to give me an income."

It is very difficult to get this type of person to change the thinking of a lifetime, which demands that she seek "security." It is very hard to explain that government bonds are not "security." It's tragic, but these people will lose their entire stake during inflation, all the while clinging to the dual myths of security and yield. If any of you are in this category and will listen, I suggest you follow Plan Two:

(1) Forget about security and yield, for they no longer exist. Keep enough cash or government bonds to pay for your running expenses for the next year and divide the remaining $160,000 as follows.

(2) Buy a bungalow in the suburbs. In most areas this is still possible for $75,000. If you can stand it mentally, mortgage it, but if this is too painful, pay for it outright.

(3) Put all the rest of your money into gold, divided as follows: 10% in Krugerrand, 60% in bullion and the balance in one of the top U.S. gold stocks.

(4) When your cash runs out and you need money for living expenses, sell your gold but only as you need it. This way your money will last much longer than it will in its current situation.

Plan Three

My third category of reader is young, in his early twenties, bright, ambitious, just starting out in his career and with just a few thousand dollars to work with. To this person I recommend Plan Three:

Take a chance. You may lose your stake and have to start again, but this is the one time in your life when you will be able to take that chance. I was in this category twenty-five years ago and I took a chance with my stake and won. As a result, I have lived like a prince ever since. If you lose, you won't be that far behind where you are now; but if you win, your whole future will be changed. I think the best chance today is in the futures market. With $2,500 you can purchase one hundred ounces of gold for delivery in one year at a price of $430. You might lose the $2,500, but with a little luck you may make many times that amount.

Why Are There So Many Books on Investing?

Every year dozens of new books come out, each giving a different formula on how to get rich. They all seem to do well—at least for their authors and publishers. But I think the public must get very confused. Who is to be believed?

In the 1960's a dance instructor named Nicholas Darvas wrote his story of *How I Made Two Million Dollars in the Stock Market.*[1] Buyers of the book discovered that the author's chief tool was to put in orders to sell stocks if they went down and to hold his winners that were going up. But those who tried to follow Darvas' method lost money as the market whipsawed.

[1] New York: American Research Council, 1960.

Ten years later Harry Browne in his *How to Profit from a Monetary Crisis*[2] advised the purchase of gold, Swiss francs, a house in the country, a supply of canned goods and a gun to fight off the neighbors once the rioting began. Poor Harry's timing couldn't have been worse. There have been no riots and his recommended gold purchase came just as gold ownership became legal in the United States and the metal's price plummeted. Harry Browne profited from his experience, and in his 1978 book, *New Profits from the Monetary Crisis*,[3] was not so certain about the future, suggesting that gold and foreign currencies might go in either direction.

Recently, Andrew Tobias in *The Only Investment Guide You'll Ever Need*[4] warned against buying "antique cars, wine, autographs, stamps, coins, diamonds, art" for two reasons: (1) You are competing against experts. (2) These things don't pay dividends and are hard for an amateur to sell because there is such a spread between retail and wholesale.

In 1978 there was even a college professor, Don Abrams, who published a book on stock market advice called *The Profit Takers*,[5] in which his entire strategy consisted of buying convertible bonds and simultaneously selling short stock in the same company, a plan certain to enrich brokers if not investors. The author calmly assured his readers that his technique would "pluck profits from the stock market no matter how it moves—up or down." Alas, as investors who tried the system discovered, it was no panacea.

The latest guru is Howard Ruff, whose *How to Prosper*

---

[2] Toronto: McGraw-Hill, 1974. New York: Macmillan, 1974.
[3] New York: Morrow, 1978.
[4] New York: Harcourt Brace Jovanovich, 1978.
[5] New York: Deneau & Greenberg, 1978.

During the Coming Bad Years[6] is on all the current best-seller lists. Mr. Ruff forecasts an Armageddon in the United States in which riots cause a breakdown in our food-distribution system. He recommends filling your home with bags of silver and a one-year supply of dehydrated foods. Alas, these foods won't last indefinitely, and so must be periodically eaten and replaced. Mr. Ruff has apparently been doing this since 1973. Having tasted a variety of dehydrated foods, I have decided that I would rather take my chances with the rioters.

The sad fact is that most investment books are written not by millionaires who have made money in the market, but by authors who hope to make money with their advice. And as a result, much of the material in these books, no matter how well meant, is misleading or just bad advice.

The other important factor is that times are changing very rapidly. A book written just two years ago may already be out of date, while one written five years ago is entirely useless. I reread my own best seller *Anyone Can Make a Million* recently and was shocked at how dated the advice has become. Undoubtedly, this book will suffer the same fate.

In addition, no one can be right all the time. I'm proud of the recommendations in my books, which have been very close to the mark, but I am not immune from blunders. I have made two classic mistakes. In 1966 I recommended the purchase of convertible bonds, which up to then had been the perfect investment. This was followed by the simultaneous collapse of both the stock and bond markets, and with them, all too many convertible bonds. More recently, in 1971, I advised the purchase of wine for investment, following the magnificent Bordeaux vintages of 1970

[6] New York: Times Books, 1979.

and 1971. My recommendation was followed by the three horrible years of 1972, 1973 and 1974, which produced barely drinkable, let alone profitable, wine.

I had intended to make a list here of all the investment books on the market with a summation of their bad advice, but my publisher became discouraged by my first venture in the field. I did a somewhat unkind review of a new book on stock advice and challenged the author to give four specific suggestions for investments. When three of these went bust I wrote it up in my *Toronto Sun* column, and the author responded with a million-dollar lawsuit. He finally did offer to settle if I'd pay his legal expenses of $2,000. I declined his kind offer.

Another problem is that even when investment advice is correct, it may break down if too many people follow it. Thus, in *Anyone Can Make a Million* I recommended free riding, the purchase and sale of bonds and stocks without paying for them. My advice was received far too well. When thousands of investors began to practice what only a handful had done up to then, the regulating authorities passed laws eliminating free riding. Similarly, in the same book, I advised the purchase of Supertest stock at $18. It really was undervalued at that price, but not many people were able to profit from it. As my readers rushed to buy, the stock quickly moved up to $40, where it was bought out by another firm.

There is no simple road to riches. Investors want to be given uncomplicated rules that will make them rich. But there are no such firm rules because the game and its rules are constantly changing. If Harry Browne had brought his first book out four years earlier, or three years later, he would have been spectacularly correct. It was not his advice that was bad; it was his timing.

Obviously, I can't tell now how well my timing will be with this volume, but in one way this book is different from all the others. Of course it contains rules and recommendations, but they are secondary to the message I'm trying to impart: *Inflation is here—it's not going away. Get rid of paper investments. Buy equity.* My timing may be good or bad, but I know that five years down the road, no one following this advice will regret it.

It really isn't deciding whom to believe. It's a matter of examining the economic facts in the United States. If you have come to the same conclusions that I have, this book will give you some solid indication of how to protect yourself—and profit during inflation.

About the Author

Dr. Morton Shulman has been deeply involved in the investment business for twenty-five years. He was president of a stock option firm in the 1950's. In 1966 his first book, *Anyone Can Make a Million*, recommended the purchase of gold at $35 an ounce. In 1973 his second investment book recommended the purchase of silver at $1.40 an ounce.

His non-business career has included four years as Chief Coroner for Toronto and two terms in the Ontario Legislature. He is at present a syndicated columnist and host of a weekly television show. He is a medical doctor.